AMOS

HOSEA

James M. Ward

KNOX PREACHING GUIDES
John H. Hayes, Editor

John Knox Press
ATLANTA

Library of Congress Cataloging in Publication Data

Ward, James Merrill, 1928 –
   Amos, Hosea.

   (Knox Preaching Guides)
   Bibliography: p.
   1. Bible. O.T. Amos—Criticism, interpretation, etc.
2. Bible. O.T. Hosea—Criticism, interpretation, etc.
3. Bible. O.T. Amos—Homiletical use.
4. Bible. O.T. Hosea—Homiletical use. I. Title.
II. Series.
BS1585.2.W29   224'.606   81-8460
ISBN 0-8042-3225-3   AACR2

© copyright John Knox Press 1981
10 9 8 7 6 5 4 3 2 1
Printed in the United States of America
John Knox Press
Atlanta, Georgia 30365

Contents

HOSEA

AMOS

Introduction

The influence of Amos in Western religion has been enormous. Probably no book of the OT has received more attention in our time in classroom and pulpit. One reason for its popularity is historical: it is the oldest surviving collection of oracles attributable to an individual Israelite prophet. Another reason is rhetorical: the oracles are powerful, clear and memorably worded, and they deal in a straightforward way with some of the most basic issues of religious ethics. For many modern teachers of the Bible, Amos stands as the prototype of classical Hebrew prophecy. There is considerable merit in the high estimate generally made of Amos' place in the history of Israelite religion. Although OT scholars today do not regard him as the first true monotheist in Israel or the pioneer of ethical religion (estimates frequently made by critics of previous generations), they do accord him a prominent role in the development of prophetic theology and literature. The older view presupposed that the Pentateuch (Genesis to Deuteronomy) was later than Amos and theologically dependent upon him and the other eighth century prophets. However, most commentators today believe that the traditions embodied in the Pentateuch took shape long before Amos and that his proclamation was rooted in the understanding of faith and morality which is expressed in the great narrative traditions of the Pentateuch. Amos is not diminished by this shift in historical judgment. On the contrary he is made more understandable by it. In the older view, he was a proponent of novel ideas which his audience could not have been expected to share and which placed them under no sense of moral obligation. In the current view, he was the defender of an ancient faith and moral commitment which he shared with his audience. He spoke from within Israel's religious tradition, not from without. Thus, he was a representative witness of the faith which his Israelite contemporaries could have been expected to affirm. In this sense Amos' ministry resembles that of the modern preacher who speaks from a position of responsibility within a congregation.

If Amos spoke as an insider in some respects, there were other respects in which he spoke as an outsider. His home was in the southern kingdom of Judah (Tekoa), yet he spoke in the northern kingdom of Israel. Further, he was inexperienced as a prophet, yet he stepped forward boldly to challenge the leadership of the national sanctuaries. For Amos, "Israel" must have meant the whole people of the covenant, comprising the twelve traditional tribes. Therefore, when God called him to prophesy to his "people Israel" (7:15), he felt entitled to do so in Bethel and Samaria, in the Kingdom of Israel. The sense of unity of all the tribes of Israel as one people of God may have been older and more fundamental than the political division into two kingdoms, or even the political unification under David and Solomon, but the priest Amaziah, at least, regarded Amos as an outsider (7:10– 14). For him Amos' Judean residency was more important than his Yahwistic calling.

Whether Amos was a layman or a professional has been much debated. His brief reply to Amaziah's dismissal (7:14) is the only evidence we have to go on, and it is ambiguous. Some scholars take it to mean that he was not a professional prophet, even though he was a prophet, while other commentators take it to mean that he was not a prophet at all, but a layman. In either case, we may rightly discern in the confrontation between Amos and Amaziah a tension between the established professional leaders in the Israelite sanctuaries and the one whom they deemed an outsider.

Thus, if certain features of Amos' experience are taken as determinative, he may be regarded as a model for prophetic voices within the religious community. However, if certain other aspects of his experience are stressed, he can serve as a model for the secular critic of religion. Both kinds of prophets can serve the truth of God, and Amos would probably have been pleased to know that his oracles would provide inspiration to both, throughout the history of western culture.

The rulers of Israel appear to have been the primary audience of Amos and Hosea; however, this category included not only the kings but also government officials, priests, and elders, in short, the upper class of the nation. The prophets often included others in their purview, sometimes, indeed, the entire nation, but they gave principal attention to the leaders.

Amos was a shepherd from Tekoa. He may have been rich or poor, literate or not, of high station or low, self-taught or schooled in the prophetic tradition. Whatever may have been the case, he produced masterful oracles. Most of his oracles are short and in poetry. There is one longer composition in the book: the oracle concerning the nations (1:1 – 2:16). The series of visions in 7:1 – 9 and 8:1 – 3 is also an extended literary unity. The remaining oracles are quite brief and seemingly independent of one another. No overall design of the book is discernible. At the same time, we have no objective basis for rearranging the order of materials. Therefore, in the treatment which follows we will deal with the materials in their canonical order. We have divided the text into twelve sections. Some of these contain more than one oracle. We have made the divisions insofar as possible in order to achieve thematic unity and manageable length. Since any such division must be arbitrary at some points, each section should be studied in relation to those adjacent to it, and indeed, to the entire book.

The historical setting of Amos' ministry was the reign of Jeroboam II of Israel (1:1). We are told that he prophesied "two years before the earthquake," but we do not know when that was. The reign of Jeroboam is described briefly in 2 Kings 14:23 – 29. Jeroboam stood in the line of Jehu, who destroyed the house of Ahab and usurped the throne of Israel (2 Kings 9 – 10). The reader can get the best sense of the historical background of Amos' career by reading the account of the last hundred years of the Kingdom of Israel in 2 Kings 1 – 17. The stories of conflict between King Ahab and the prophets Elijah and Micaiah (1 Kings 19 – 22) will also throw light upon the similar conflict between the house of Jeroboam and the prophet Amos.

The main thing to realize in setting the historical context of Amos, as compared with that of Hosea, is that Amos' work seems to have been done entirely before the era of Israel's collapse, while Hosea's extended into that era. Amos' time was one of prosperity, but Hosea's was already one of adversity for the Kingdom of Israel.

Many Nations, One Justice (1:1 – 2:16)

Oracles of judgment seldom fall on willing ears. Therefore, prophets are unpopular and their books are hard to preach. Who of us wants to receive a cold blast from Amos or Jeremiah? We don't go to church for that. There is enough bad news swirling around us the rest of the time. Consequently, a preacher must use special care to hold people's attention if the prophetic message is really to be heard.

Sometimes a prophetic book supplies its own means of winning the hearer's attention. The intriguing story of Hosea's marriage and the vivid biography of Jeremiah provide narrative settings for their words which engage people's interest at once. Amos' encounter with the priest Amaziah (7:10–17) does this, too. Other clues are internal to the oracles themselves. This is the case in the text before us. The punch line of this sermon is a denunciation of Amos' audience for social injustice (2:6–16). But the people's attention is engaged by the "lead-in," which is a denunciation of rival nations (1:3–2:5). The judgment against these other peoples is not a fiction, devised merely as a clever way to introduce the real message. It, too, is a serious word, and it has important theological implications. But it does serve as an effective rhetorical device.

The same device could be used by the modern preacher, whether preaching on this text or some other. One can imagine other communities similar to one's own congregation, which can be criticized in the light of the prophetic ethic. The audience will get the message, without the preacher's having to harp on their own situation.

The masterful literary construction of Amos' oracle is another reason for its rhetorical effectiveness, and is another feature of this text which the modern preacher can study with profit. The repetition of the provocative introduction ("For the three transgressions of . . .") gives rhythmic pace to the recitation, creating an emotional crescendo. Martin Luther

King used a similar device powerfully in his preaching. Recall the famous speech in which he kept repeating, "I have a dream. . . ." Note also Amos' use of one basic form in each of the component parts, with just enough variation to keep the recital from becoming boring. And then note the economy of words. These are some of the literary means which the prophet has employed to make his communication effective.

There are many oracles of judgment against foreign nations in the Bible, including whole sections of the major prophetic books (Isa 13 – 23; Jer 46 – 51; Ezek 25 – 32). It is not surprising that these are there, for the biblical writers believed that God's righteous rule extended to all the world. Denunciations of other peoples can be dangerous, however, for they tempt us into self-righteousness and the comfortable illusion that God is on our side against our enemies. Many of the oracles against foreign nations in the Bible fail to provide safeguards against this temptation. Indeed, they may appear to some readers to be blatantly nationalistic. By contrast, Amos 1:3 – 2:16 delivers its hardest blows to the Israelite audience itself. This is one reason why it is perhaps the greatest oracle of its kind in the Bible.

We don't know exactly where or when Amos delivered this great oracle on the nations, but it is possible to imagine a likely setting. Picture a major religious celebration in Bethel, the national sanctuary of the Kingdom of Israel. Thousands of people would be gathered in expectation of an experience of personal and communal renewal. The promises of God would be reappropriated and the people's good fortune reaffirmed. Somewhere in the course of the proceeding a prophet would proclaim an oracle against foreign nations. It would be in a traditional form, like all such liturgical utterances. The purpose would be to invoke God's judgment upon Israel's rivals and secure her claims against them. Therefore, when Amos began his arresting proclamation against Israel's neighbors, the first response of his audience would have been one of enthusiastic approval. The negative response illustrated by the priest Amaziah (7:10 – 17) would have come only as Amos changed the direction of his denunciation and aimed it toward Israel herself.

If this reconstruction of the setting of his oracle is correct, it means that Amos was speaking from within the cultic com-

munity—the religious establishment—and not from outside
it. Amos, like the other prophets of the OT, was not a misanthropic outsider, condemning an institution which he neither
cared about nor understood, but a concerned insider, calling
the community (and himself) to responsible behavior.

We have already noted two important teachings of this
text. The first is that God's justice is universal. All peoples are
held accountable for their treatment of each other, and can expect to suffer punishment at the hand of God for cruelty and
oppression. The second is that Israel—the "people of God"—is
subject to the same demand and the same punishment as
others. Their religion does not give them special status in
God's eyes.

Next we should examine the actual behavior which Amos
condemns in this oracle. The crimes of the non-Israelites are
acts of violence against other peoples. Specifically, they are
physical cruelty (1:3), enslavement of persons (1:6, 9), insatia-
ble violence (1:11), and murder of defenseless women (1:13).
Breach of treaty (1:9) is also mentioned, as is an obscure act
involving the bones of an Edomite king (2:1). Thus, most of
these crimes are obvious and extreme violations of human life
and basic human rights. Amos' audience would have recog-
nized them instantly for what they were and condemned the
perpetrators just as severely as the prophet did.

Israel's own crimes, as Amos catalogued them, were not
as obvious or extreme as the others', but he judged his people
just as severely as he did the foreign nations. The first injustice that he named is debt-slavery (2:6). Next, apparently, is
denial of the legal rights of the poor and weak (2:7). Then
come sexual exploitation of women (the exact circumstances
are unclear, though sacred prostitution may be meant), misappropriation of pledges and fines levied upon the poor (2:8),
and abuse of persons with special religious callings (2:12).

As we read the Bible and try to appropriate its message in
our own time, we should not expect to see ourselves and our
world mirrored exactly in the ancient texts. However, it is
possible to see similar things going on in our lives and around
us and thus to heed Amos' criticism and his warning.

Our society does not permit debt-slavery, and our religious communities do not practice sacred prostitution, but
beneath the surface of these evils lie distortions of human re-

lationships which have parallels in our society. In the first case, we can see in our own world stronger, wealthier people willing to gain their own economic advantage at the cost of the freedom and dignity of weaker, poorer people, and willing to perpetuate economic structures in which such oppression is a regular occurrence. In the second case, we can observe the debasement of persons through mechanical and commercial sex. Amos didn't say whether he regarded the user or the used as the greater victim, but we may observe that both suffer from such depersonalization of sexual intimacy. Thus a great human good is distorted and made destructive.

To turn to Amos' next charge, namely that of judicial injustice (2:7–8), we can observe today ways in which the poor and disfranchised are deprived of equal justice with the comfortable and highly placed. Our system of criminal justice is theoretically blind to distinctions of race and class, but often the poor cannot afford the judicial processes available to others, and they do not always receive the same kind of treatment by the police.

We do not have prophets and Nazirites of the ancient sort (2:11) in our modern religious communities, but we are subject to the same kinds of prejudice, fear, and self-interest that caused the persecution of such persons in Israel. The issue here is *religious* persecution. We may pride ourselves that our society is overtly free of this, but religious prejudice infects our lives in many ways. Anti-Semitism is not dead, although it has taken subtle forms in many quarters. Ridicule of others is still commonplace, though today it is directed less often at persons of other religious denominations than at those whose style of religious expression and celebration differs from our own: "evangelical" vs. "liberal" or "charismatic" vs. "conventional," for example. The OT prophets were severely critical of religious practices which they observed, but these were practices within *their own* religious community, not someone else's. Amos did not condemn the foreign nations for having alien styles of worship. He condemned them for oppression of human beings.

The evils Amos described were all crimes against persons. They were committed in international conflict, and in his view they would be punished in the same arena. Thus, the general principle that seems to be articulated here is that na-

tions which live by the sword can expect in the justice of God
to die by the sword. In general the experience of the nations of
the Middle East in Amos' time bears ample testimony to the
truth of this conviction. Here, as almost everywhere else in the
book of Amos, the threatened punishment fits the crime. Both
are military-political. There is no linking of moral causes and
non-moral effects. The punishments are not natural calamities imposed by God arbitrarily from without. They are social
calamities taking place within the historical process itself, by
means of the interactions of nations and peoples.

God's judgment against moral evil is not the only word
the prophets spoke, but it was the most frequent and often the
first. It is also an essential ingredient in any authentic Christian proclamation. As long as human injustice exists, the true
prophet will declare God's judgment against it. This judgment is not opposed to God's love but is required by it, for the
sake of the ultimate well-being of both the oppressed and the
oppressor. The Christian preacher may wish to make his first
word that of the good news of the Gospel, and he will certainly
wish to ground his entire message in that good news, but unless he is willing to make a sober appraisal of the moral situation in which he speaks, and to address the evils that beset it,
the good news he brings will be superficial. The OT prophets
provide a constant reminder of the moral seriousness of all
true biblical preaching, and much of the content of their oracles has a direct or indirect applicability to the life of religious
communities in all ages.

According to the Bible, God is champion of the oppressed
and judge of the oppressor. Neither receives perfect justice all
the time, for God does not manipulate human lives. In the actual course of history the oppressors may be brought down
more surely than the oppressed are raised up. The latter event
requires constructive human action. The former results from
the perennial rivalries of nations. It is this judgment against
doers of injustice to which Amos points in the present oracle.
The other, positive aspect of God's justice, namely the fulfillment of human life, is not as explicit a theme in prophetic oracles. However, it is presupposed by them. And it should be the
equal concern of religious communities in our own time.

It would be easy to adapt the eight-fold oracle in Amos
1:3 – 2:16 to the situation of modern worshippers, as a kind of

litany of prophetic reflection. Merely substitute for the names of the ancient nations those of modern nations, communities, political parties, or other entities, which may be perceived by the congregation as competitive or hostile toward them, and toward the values they hold dear. For Israel, in the climactic oracle, substitute "us"!

This section of Amos contains numerous possibilities for preaching. Several have already been mentioned. Here is one possible treatment:

First, God's justice is universal. All nations and communities are subject to the same righteous rule. Religious communities experience this divine justice in the same way other communities do.

Second, the righteous judgments of God are effected within the historical process itself. Rewards and punishments are experienced within and through the interactions of peoples and groups; they are not "supernatural."

Third, rewards and punishments do not always work out exactly as nations or groups deserve. God's justice is not mechanical. There is great flexibility in human interaction because of the freedom which God has given us. Therefore, our commitment must be to justice for all people, not because we will be rewarded for it, but because it is right in God's eyes.

Religious Knowledge and Moral Accountability
(3:1 – 2; 9:7 – 10)

Historical allusions are infrequent in Amos. This reference to the exodus from Egypt is unusual, but it carries a telling message. It says that responsibility is inseparable from blessing. Israel and her heirs, ancient and modern, have not always understood this. The temptation is to seek blessing and shun responsibility. One way of doing this is to formalize responsibility into a set of religious rituals and then maintain them rigorously in the expectation of special divine favor. There are some devastating comments on this sort of behavior in later sections of Amos (4:4 – 5; 5:21 – 24). The present section deals with the religious attitude lying behind such behavior, that is, the conviction that Israel could expect special blessing because she had a unique relationship to God. This belief is cited explicitly in 3:1, where the point is reinforced by using the special Israelite name for God, "Yahweh" ("LORD,"

RSV). The same understanding is implied in 1:9–10. What Amos repudiated was the morally vicious notion that God gave Israel immunity from divine judgment as a consequence of her special covenantal relationship. He declared, instead, that of all the peoples of the world Israel could expect most to be held accountable for her evil deeds. No other nation was immune from God's righteous judgment—Amos had already made this clear in the great opening section of the book. But, Israel was immune least of all.

Amos 3:1–2 should be read together with 9:7–10, for much the same point is made in the two passages: God's providential guidance of Israel means that she can expect to suffer the moral consequences of her unrighteous acts. God does not exempt his own people from the operation of his justice in the course of human history.

At the same time, these two passages appear to contradict each other with regard to the question of Israel's special relationship to God. Amos 3:1–2 seems to acknowledge the uniqueness of this relationship (while denying the conclusion that it gives Israel immunity from divine punishment), but 9:7 seems to be saying that Israel's relationship to God is not different from that of other nations. However, on closer examination we may be able to resolve the apparent contradiction.

Amos 3:2 locates the uniqueness of Israel's relationship with God in a uniqueness of *knowledge*. Although God may have guided the other nations in their historic development (9:7), Israel is the only nation he has known (3:2).

There are as many kinds of knowing in the language of the OT as in our own, and in the one as in the other it is impossible to appeal here to some supposed technical sense of the word in order to make our point. We can only say that the best sense that can be made of Amos' assertion, when we take it in relation to what he says elsewhere about Israel and the other nations, is that he is speaking here about *mutual* knowledge, that is, a relationship in which Israel is known by God and also knows him. If this is the correct interpretation, it means that the only difference between the people of God and the peoples of the world is one of religious knowledge. Israel's faith in the one God is all that sets her apart. This distinctive faith has many consequences for the understanding of human existence, but one of the most important is a deepened and expanded sense of accountability to God. Amos felt it. Apparently, many in Israel did not.

The word Amos proclaimed, at the moment in Israel's history when he felt compelled to speak, was a word of divine judgment. But this was not the only message contained in the tradition which he embraced. This tradition also contained the word of God's gracious guidance of the destinies of nations (9:7). It was not the word Amos felt compelled to speak to an insensitive nation, which took grace for granted and forgot responsibility, but it was an essential part of the total prophetic witness, and it would become compelling to other spokesmen of God in other circumstances. It, too, is a word not to be forgotten by the people of God.

Because of Israel's moral insensitivity, Amos drew the negative conclusion from the linking of knowledge and accountability: those who know God can expect his punishment of their evil ways. Other OT texts, which are related in import to Amos 3:2, draw the positive conclusion: God makes himself known to Israel so that she may follow his ways and receive the blessing that is inherent in them (Gen 18:19 and Hos 13:5).

Like Amos 3:2, these passages in Genesis and Hosea relate the message of knowledge and responsibility to the story of the fathers and the exodus from Egypt, for this story is the central locus of Israel's religious tradition. Israel's knowledge of God is rooted in the story of salvation, which stretches from the call of Abraham (Gen 12) to the settlement in the land of promise. This is a story of both judgment and blessing, and it provided rich resources for the prophets' preaching, just as their oracles provide further resources for preaching in our time.

For the prophets, the knowledge of God was not merely something for Israel to enjoy. It was something to live out of. Not a private religious experience, but the basis of human interaction and the ground of communal formation.

It is significant that Amos refers to the whole "family" of Israel (3:1) as the ones known by God. The term "family" is in danger of becoming a cliché in modern religious usage. Nevertheless, to think of Israel as a family is a central concept of the Bible. The Hebrew word covers more than the nuclear family (wife, husband and children), although it certainly includes it. It can refer to extensive kinship groups, and thus is a reasonable metaphor to apply to the wider community of Israel. In the present case the reference is not to blood relationship but to mutual attachment and mutual obligation. To call a nation (or a religious denomination) of several million people a "family" may seem like a mockery. However, even though it is partly an unrealizable ideal, it is an ideal that can be actualized in human sentiment and behavior, and it is the ultimate standard by which deeds and relationships are measured. Therefore, it can motivate action and reform even when it is not fully or permanently realized. Of all the metaphors of the Bible, this one of the family is the most satisfactory for describing the intention of God's covenant with Israel and the nature of the people of God and can provide today's minister with sermonic possibilities. Hosea employed family language much more extensively than did Amos, as we shall see in the second half of this book; but Amos obviously accepted this way of understanding Israel, also.

Family relationships are deeply personal, engaging the heart as well as the mind and will. Obligation is not imposed upon them from without but flows naturally from an intense, inward caring. One simply feels oneself responsible to and for the other family members. And one's own wellbeing, happiness, and fulfillment are inextricably bound up with theirs. Furthermore, there is no limit to this involvement in each other's lives, this pervasive sense of responsibility, of belonging to each other. It extends to every facet of life, and it never ends. This is the ideal of covenantal existence for Israel and for all those who count themselves among Israel's heirs.

Nothing set Israel apart from other nations in the providence of God except her religious faith, her knowledge of God. She could not expect greater material prosperity or preferred treatment in the execution of divine justice. But the knowledge of God is a supreme gift! To know God truly is to perceive the truth about the world, about human beings, about oneself. So, in this sense, it makes all the difference! But to misconstrue Israel's special relationship to God in any other terms is to misunderstand God's nature and thus to undermine the very knowledge which defined Israel's being. To do this was a constant temptation in Amos' time, just as it is in our own.

The idea of special providence has played an important part in American life. We have believed our system of government, our economy, and our way of life to be guided by the hand of God, and we have often interpreted them as the just rewards for the superior virtue of the American people. It is not necessary to deny the genuine values in the culture or the natural goodness of the land in order to recognize the self-righteousness—and self-deception—in this attitude. It is as foolish today as it was in ancient Israel, and the arrogance and complacency which it breeds are just as vicious. The gifts are undeserved, to be received in gratitude and moral commitment, but without any self-congratulation.

Who are the modern equivalents—for us—of the Ethiopians, Philistines, and Syrians of Amos 9:7? Not our enemies or rivals, so much, for Israel was not on hostile terms with these peoples in Amos' time, but simply other peoples—any other peoples. Nations, if we are thinking of our nation; religious faiths, if we are thinking of our own communion; ethnic groups; or social classes; the other sex; the stranger; the outsider; "they." And the point to remember—to be reminded of, over and over again—is that these people are as much the object of God's concern as we are. Objects of his righteous demands and of his providential care.

These short passages contain a rich message. One sermon cannot do full justice to it. Two possible lines of approach might be called outer and inner, or national and personal. In the first we could consider the relationship of God to the nations, peoples, or churches of the world. Here the main point is that God *both* guides and judges *both* Israel ("us") and other peoples. Other peoples receive the same kind of providential care that God extends to his covenantal people (9:7– 10). Secondly, the covenantal people cannot expect only blessing from God. On the contrary, they are held especially accountable to God for disobedience or infidelity. Israel has surer *knowledge* than other nations of God's universal guidance and justice, because of her faith in the one, transcendent Creator. Therefore, she has an advantage in understanding. However, she has no material or political advantage over any other of God's peoples.

The interior approach to Amos 3:1– 2 could stress the clause "You only have I known of all the families of the earth." Knowing, in religious, covenantal terms means *mutual* knowledge; it involves the *mind and will* as well as the heart; it is *re-*

sponsible to all those who share the covenant relationship; and this responsibility, like that within a *family*, is unlimited in the *range* of what it involves (it deals with the whole person) and unlimited in *duration* ("love never ends"). The rewards and punishments which are experienced in such a relationship are personal and intrinsic, not material and extrinsic. Infidelity brings loss of trust, love, fellowship, and mutual support, while faithfulness brings the fulfillment of these things.

Action and Reaction (3:3 –8)

Amos wrote little about himself. A few facts are recorded in the dialogue with the priest Amaziah (7:10 –17) and in the editorial superscription to the book (1:1). This is all. Some think the present passage is Amos' interpretation of the motive and meaning of his call to prophesy. As a report of his own call, it adds little to what is said in 7:14 –15. Its significance lies elsewhere. It expresses the urgency of prophesying at the moment of divine command (3:8), and it advocates a theory concerning the relation of prophetic interpretation to historical event (3:7). It also shows how analogies from nature and human experience can be used in preaching, to capture attention and stimulate thought (3:1 –6).

The tantalizing questions in this passage tumble over each other so the mind can hardly keep up. It is like listening to an orchestral crescendo. One tries to catch the inner voices of the music but is carried along by the mounting climax of the dominant theme. Here, too, in Amos' proclamation, the main statement is the last: "The Lord Yahweh has spoken; who would not prophesy?!" Compelled by divine command, Amos must speak, whether or not (this is the tacit assumption) the people want to listen. His speaking is not for nothing, mere idle chatter. His action is in reality a reaction to God. It is not at his own initiative.

Reading this today we find it easy to accept Amos' assertion, for everyone knows Amos was a prophet! His oracles are right there in the Bible! But it wasn't easy for Amos' hearers to accept. There wasn't any Bible then! It may be that God speaks through prophets, but how do you recognize a genuine prophet when you hear one? Surely not everyone who claims to be a prophet is one. Nothing in Amos' speech helps answer this question. It shows only that *he* was convinced he was speaking for God. How can this conviction be tested?

The OT mentions several ways of distinguishing true from false prophecy. One test is that of history. If a prophecy comes to pass, it is a genuine word of God, and if it doesn't, it isn't (Deut 18:22). This test has a certain value, for it may provide a basis for evaluating the course of a people's history and learning from prior experience. Therefore, we should not dismiss it entirely as a criterion of true prophecy. Nevertheless, it provides no help at the time an ostensible prophet is speaking.

Another test is that the proclamation must be in the name of the Lord, Yahweh, and not in the name of another deity (Deut 18:20; 13:1–11). The analogy for Christians today would be speaking in the name of Christ, or "the God and Father of our Lord Jesus Christ," rather than, say, the Buddha, or Deity as conceived in Buddhism. Applying this test to religious proclamation would not mean that nothing in Buddhism could be accepted by Christians as true. It would mean, rather, that the standard of judgment of what is true is the gospel of Jesus Christ and not Buddhist teaching itself. Many things in Buddhist teaching may prove to be compatible with Christian faith, but their truth is judged in the light of Jesus Christ, and not the other way around.

So far, so good. But what about claims and counterclaims among those who believe they *are* speaking in the name of Christ? Or, in the case of Amos' contemporaries, the Lord Yahweh? The Book of Amos provides no explicit guidelines for dealing with this problem, although much that is said there has an implicit bearing upon it.

We need to distinguish here between two kinds of prophetic assertion. The first is the prediction of an impending event which is viewed as an act of God, especially a divine judgment. The second is the accusation of ethical or religious wrongdoing, with or without an accompanying appeal for moral reform. When we speak about tests of prophecy we are inclined to mean tests of predictive prophecy; however, the test provided in Deut 13:1–11 has much more to do with the ethical content of prophetic proclamation. The false prophet is one who leads the people away from Yahweh, the God of the Covenant, and from the moral and religious responsibilities that go with faith in him. On the other hand, a

prophet who announces a coming act of God which never
comes to pass is deluded, and therefore, according to Deut
18:22, is not a true spokesman for God. Since the prophetic
books contain both announcements of impending judgment
and moral criticism, both tests of prophecy must be taken
into account. Therefore, when Amos declares the necessity of
prophesying for the Lord Yahweh (3:8), we may rightly infer
that both aspects of prophecy are meant, and not merely the
announcement of judgment.

But now, when we examine the other major assertion contained in this passage, namely, that "the Lord Yahweh does
nothing without revealing his plans to his servants the
prophets" (3:7), we appear to be dealing only with the predictive element of prophecy. Some commentators attribute v. 7
to a later editor of the book, partly because the theological assertion made in it is different from what is suggested by the
rest of the oracle. Nevertheless, we must take account of what
is said there.

Is it true that God never acts without first disclosing
through a prophet what he is planning to do? What would
such a claim imply with regard to the interpretation of history? Are all historical events acts of God, or only some of them?
Which ones? Since there are many events in history which are
not announced by prophets, either the assertion in 3:7 is
wrong, or it means something else by acts of God than the ordinary succession of historical events.

We should not feel compelled to defend the truth of every
statement in the Bible. The biblical message of faith in God
can stand up perfectly well even though there are errors in
human judgment, knowledge, or perception reflected in the
biblical writings. The modern reader need not be defensive
about such things. Nevertheless, we should try to understand
what is said, and give it a chance to claim our assent before we
judge it to be wrong.

There is an interesting ambiguity in Amos 3:7. The phrase
"does nothing" might also be translated "establishes no
word," since the Hebrew word in question means both
"word" and "thing." One possible connotation of the sentence, then, is that prophetic proclamation is an essential ingredient in the accomplishment of any word of God. Not that
prophets have advance knowledge of every happening that

falls within the sovereignty of God, but that their speaking is the means of God's communication. If it is necessary for a prophet of God to interpret God's purpose to his people (3:7), then, indeed, "Who would not prophesy" (3:8) when this word is given to him? Understood in this way, Amos 3:7– 8 hangs together. Not every act of God requires a prophet. But if an historical event is to be a *meaningful* act of God, it must be interpreted in the light of the prophetic faith.

What meaning does this assertion have for the modern Church? It puts a heavy responsibility upon the ministers and other representatives of the Church to interpret human affairs in the light of the word of God. If the course of our life is to be understood as in any sense an unfolding of the righteous purpose of God, then there must be "prophets" who will venture to speak for God. What message they are to declare is not the question raised by this passage. It is merely that there must be those who are willing to speak for God. This is a risky business, without guarantees, but it is essential to the very existence of the people of God.

It would be arrogant to claim that the only prophets of God are within the Church. Others outside the Church—poets, artists, journalists, political leaders, scientists, many more— may serve this function from time to time. But there must be those within the Church who carry the perennial responsibility of prophetic preaching. Otherwise, the Church ceases to be the Church.

God needs prophetic interpreters of his way and his will, and he summons men and women to fulfill this ministry. Like Amos of old, his ministers will feel compelled to speak, both by the urgency of the situation and by the insistence of the divine call. Without such voices the word of God's judgment against injustice remains unspoken, and the word of invitation to the way of righteousness remains unheard. Let those who have heard God's judging and saving word repeat it for the sake of all!

Precarious Privilege (3:9– 4:3)

Rural poor people may disdain or condemn the urban rich, and we may attempt to dismiss their criticism as envy or "sour grapes." Amos was a herdsman from a little town in Judah (1:1; 7:14), and in the series of brief oracles that come next in the book (3:9 – 4:3) he attacked the rich and powerful in Samaria, capital of the Kingdom of Israel. Was there a measure of envy in his attitude? A note of class-rivalry? Possibly. Those whom he attacked would probably have thought so, and used the thought as a rationalization for their privileged status. However, ancient Israel was a closer-knit society than our own. The social distance between people was not as great and the claims of one segment of the community upon another could not be put out of mind so easily. A persistent prophet could eventually get attention. The situation was closer to that which exists within a modern church, or denomination, than the one which exists within a large nation like our own.

If a modern church is more like ancient Israel in size and social cohesion than a modern nation is, it is less like Israel as a political entity. The people whom Amos addressed in these oracles were privileged and powerful in both the religious community and the nation. These two realms—religion and politics, or church and state—were not separated in ancient society as they are in our own. Therefore, it would be unfair of the modern preacher to apply Amos' teaching in any simple way to the life of an American congregation. We need to acknowledge the differences candidly, as well as the resulting difficulty in preaching from texts like these.

There are four short oracles in Amos 3:9 – 4:3. Amos 3:9 – 11 is a mock summons to the armies of Assyria and Egypt to examine the social oppression, violence and crime within Samaria, capital of Israel—evils perpetrated by the powerful against the weak—and then to destroy the city for its crimes. Amos 3:12 predicts that only bits and pieces of Samaria will be left after its conquest. Amos 3:13 – 15 threatens the destruction of the palaces and royal temples of Israel as a punishment of God. Amos 4:1 – 3 satirizes the self-indulgent wealthy women of Israel (the "cows of Bashan") and threatens them with humiliation in the day of disaster. Each of these short pieces is an independent saying, but they deal with a common theme.

Amos prophesied the military conquest of the nation of Israel by Assyria or Egypt, and interpreted it as God's punishment of the Israelite leadership for their self-indulgence and their oppression of the poor. Such a prophecy poses several questions for us. Can we agree with Amos that the conquest of Israel by a foreign power was the result of social injustice within the Israelite community? Secondly, can we make any similar correlation in our own time between a nation's internal social conditions and its external political affairs?

On the first question, I think we should admit that the OT prophets oversimplified the actual course of Israel's history. More factors were involved in determining her destiny among the kingdoms of the world than how the powerful rich treated the powerless poor within Israel. The most important determinant of her treatment at the hands of the great powers was whether her rulers accepted the vassal status forced upon them by the major kingdoms and paid their regular tribute. What went on in the sanctuaries, markets, and law courts of Israel had slight influence, if any, upon her military and political fortunes. The link which the prophets believed to exist between internal moral conditions and external political conditions was not as strong as they supposed, even though these realms may not have been entirely independent of one another.

When we turn to the second question, we find even greater difficulty in applying the prophets' understanding of history. There may be an indirect connection between the quality of justice within a modern nation and its place among the other nations of the world, but, if so, it is far from obvious what it might be. There are so many variables involved, politically, economically, socially, technologically, that any generalization in this regard would be dubious. Geo-politics are so complex today that the simple moral formulas of ancient prophets seem irrelevant to our world.

Is this aspect of the prophetic message unpreachable, then, in the twentieth century? This conclusion would be too extreme. Although the prophets' view of the relation between social justice and political conquest in ancient Israel does not provide an adequate basis for understanding contemporary world history, their proclamation does contain elements which can be affirmed today in Christian or Jewish preaching, notably the concern for social justice and the criticism of selfish privilege. These remain valid perennially for the people of God.

By presenting the word of judgment against the sanctuary of Bethel (3:14– 15) together with the indictment of rich Samarians for self-indulgence and oppression of the poor

(4:1–3), the book of Amos challenges prosperous religious congregations to question themselves about the justification of luxury in a world where many are deprived. No one else can properly decide for a congregation how it ought to allocate its budget or whether its building programs are justified in the light of the moral demands of its tradition. However, every congregation professing commitment to the biblical faith has a continual obligation to examine its activities in this regard. It is not enough to claim that what a church does is "God's work." Religion can be selfish and self-indulgent, both in ancient Israel and in modern America. Prophetic criticism of religion is perennially necessary. This criticism is most effective when it is self-administered by a religious community. In the absence of such self-criticism, an Amos may arise to speak the judging, saving word.

In preaching on Amos 3:9–4:3 today, the emphasis should be upon the attitudes and behavior of privileged persons within our society and of privileged congregations in the church. Do we enjoy a greater share of the world's wealth, resources, and opportunities than others in our society or in the world? Do we rationalize our self-indulgence in the name of religion? What are the likely consequences of self-indulgence in these circumstances? How can we use our resources as faithful members of God's covenant community?

Missed Opportunities (4:4–13)

Repentance can be a superficial thing, producing no permanent change in behavior. Ritual acts of contrition are sometimes like this. A formal confession is made; a ritual gesture is performed; words of absolution are spoken; a momentary sense of release from guilt is experienced; but afterward life goes on as usual.

The sacrificial system in ancient Israel was understood to provide, among other things, the means of forgiveness of sin. By itself it was an insufficient means of atoning for moral, as distinguished from merely ritual, transgressions. For moral offenses the worshippers were also required to amend their behavior, or make amends for what they had done. Reformation of life was a necessary part of true repentance. But this proper understanding of worship was often distorted, according to the testimony of the prophets. Moral seriousness was eroded by self-interest, and only a mechanical ritualism remained.

The litany in Amos 4:4– 13, which might be called a litany of impenitence, is an answer to this sort of ritualism. Formally, it appears to be an imitation of a ritual of cursing. It includes a call to worship (4:4– 5), a recital of acts of God (punctuated by a five-fold refrain, 4:6– 11), an announcement of God's judgment (4:12), and a closing doxology (4:13; see the comments on the doxologies in Amos in the discussion of 5:1– 20). But unlike the ritual of cursing, which seems to have been part of the periodic ceremony of covenant-renewal (Deut 31:9– 13; 28:1– 68), Amos' litany focuses upon past events of divine discipline rather than future threats. In so doing, it demonstrates the incorrigibility of Israel. Through a whole series of chastening events, God has provided repeated occasions for moral self-criticism and reformation. However, Israel has allowed them to pass blindly, missing every opportunity. As a result, she must finally face destruction. She has believed the sanctuary to be the place of meeting with God (4:4– 5), but the actual place is the world. And the consequence of meeting will be the opposite of what she expects. The Lord of all creation (4:13) will meet Israel, as he once did Sodom and Gomorrah, as the destroyer (4:11– 12).

The writers of the OT tended to speak about all sorts of events, both in nature and in history, as deeds of God. The idea of "nature" as a realm of self-regulating, freely interacting forces, an idea which is largely the product of modern physical science, was unknown to them. Therefore, they viewed processes and happenings in the physical world as direct manifestations of God's will. Historical events were interpreted similarly, even though in this realm the human agents were observable. Furthermore, since God was not capricious, there had to be some moral explanation of his acts. For the OT writers, this meant interpreting the fortunes of Israel as rewards for righteousness or punishments for evil. This interpretation was not always made in a simple way, indeed it was challenged by some of the biblical writers (notably, the writers of Job and Ecclesiastes). Nevertheless, it is fairly pervasive in the pages of the OT.

How shall we appropriate this passage in Amos, and related texts in the Bible? We cannot take destructive happenings in the physical world—tornadoes, drought, disease—as punishments brought about by human iniquity; nor can we take physical wellbeing or material prosperity as divine rewards for human virtue. The weight of empirical evidence against such a correlation is overwhelming. Furthermore, it violates the NT gospel of God's indiscriminate love for all his creatures (Matt 5:45). Therefore, we must look for another dimension in the prophetic message and set aside the interpretation of natural events as immediate divine judgments.

In the case of Amos 4:4– 13, one other such dimension might be called reflection on the uses of adversity. It is not necessary to explain how or why adverse experiences came about in order to use them as occasions for self-examination. A community suffering affliction may need to take stock of its life, reevaluate its goals, and examine its loyalties. Today this is called "setting priorities." A social or economic crisis may startle people out of complacency and self-interest and lead them to redirect their energies toward the common good. Persons who suffer pain and deprivation can come through the experience more responsive to the pain of others.

The view I have expressed here concerning natural calamities stands in direct opposition to the perspective of many religious people. There are many, both inside and outside the Christian Church, who believe—or fear—that disease and other forms of physical disaster are punishments of God for sin, known or unknown. This conviction produces feelings of guilt and anger toward God. It is a vicious belief. Ancient people cannot be blamed for holding it because they knew little or nothing about the causes of disease or any other phenomenon in nature. They were forced to explain physical calamities as acts of God—or of other supernatural beings, such as demons or angels. However, we do not need to resort to such an explanation, because we know enough about the processes of nature—even though there is much that we do not yet know—to perceive physical events as resulting from physical causes. Germs—and other entities and conditions in nature—cause disease, not God. And there is no empirical reason to suppose that these entities behave in response to any moral laws or supernatural direction. Like the sun which God causes to shine indiscriminately upon the evil and the good (Matt 5:45), germs attack people without any regard for their moral deserving; and God does not interfere with the activity of germs to afflict selected persons and to save others from affliction. Created beings interact with each other freely without any such divine manipulation. We simply cannot find moral causes of non-moral phenomena. Therefore, the only moral or religious question that we can legitimately ask about natural disasters is how we may respond to them constructively. How can we exercise our God-given responsibility in the face of the disaster?

According to biblical faith, devotion to God must always be expressed through love of the neighbor. Therefore, when a prophet speaks about "returning to God" (4:6, 8, 9, 10, 11), this includes recommitment to the moral principles of the covenant, and, for Amos especially, concern for the rights of the poor and the powerless. A religious revival which fails to generate new zeal for social justice has nothing to do with biblical faith. That sort of religion was condemned by the prophets as baalism, and it is equally suspect in its modern dress. Amos mocked the religious people of his day to "Come to Bethel and transgress!" The equivalent charge to us would be, "Come to church and transgress." It is a rare person in today's church who would regard any practice of religion as a moral evil. However, by prophetic standards, it is evil if it feeds self-interest, regardless of the name under which it worships God. Baalism was not rejected by the prophets merely because of its false conception of deity. It was rejected also because of its destructive impact upon society.

Amos 4:4–13 is a good illustration of the conviction, expressed often in the Bible, that God disciplines his people by means of events in her history. The basis of this discipline is God's love for Israel, coupled with his demand for righteousness. Its purpose is to bring about moral discernment, repentance, and reformation of life. Thus, God is viewed not merely as a Judge, meting out punishments to those convicted of evil, but as Parent-Teacher, patiently training them in the way of righteousness.

This notion of divine discipline is more fully developed in the oracles of Hosea and will be discussed in more detail in the second part of this book. Hosea regarded even the fall of the Kingdom of Israel as a chastening event which would lead to repentence and covenant-renewal. Amos did not look beyond the fall (if 9:8b –15 is a later addition to the book, as most scholars believe). For him, the time of discipline was coming to an end. Israel had had numerous opportunities to reorder its life, but had let them all pass unheeded.

As long as one lives, there are always new possibilities of obedience and faith within the providence of God. But while this is true of individual persons, it may not be true of groups or institutions. Kingdoms rise and fall, and so do religious communities, political parties, business and social organizations. Amos addressed a kingdom which was both a national state and a religious community. The members of a modern religious congregation participate in many kinds of institution and community: political, economic, social. None of these associations is identical to those of the ancient Israelites. Therefore, Amos' oracles should not be taken as applying in a simple, straightforward way to the circumstances or responsibilities of modern life. However, by the exercise of creative imagination, a modern congregation can find stimulus in Amos' oracles to examine its own life and loyalties. Some of what Amos said about Israel's experience under God in the eighth century B.C. may help to clarify the experience and faith of persons and societies in our own time.

This text of Amos can be preached as a sermon on three "R's"—reversal, revival, and repentance. *Reversal*: Reversals of our plans and expectations come to all of us. Usually we are concerned to understand why they have occurred or how repetitions of them might be avoided. We should also ask how we can respond constructively to them in faith. *Revival*: A common response of religious people is to renew or redouble their religious activities, that is, to engage in a revival of ritual (including prayer). If this is all we do, it may be a selfish response, with no lasting moral effect. *Repentance*: True revival includes renewal of moral commitment—seeking justice and loving the neighbor. In this quest, God's gift of new life is received, and the whole process of reversal and renewal can be seen as a God-given and God-enabled opportunity.

The Unexpected Day of the Lord (5:1 –20)

In God's providence there are frequent reversals of human expectation. "He has put down the mighty from their thrones, and exalted those of low degree" (Luke 1:52). The pre-

sent section of the book of Amos ends with the famous oracle
on the Day of the Lord, which is proclaimed as the reversal of
what Israel expects of her meetings with God. This section is
not a formally delineated unit in the text, but it has a certain
thematic unity. It opens with a lament over the fall of Israel
(5:1 –3) and closes with an announcement of the day of wrath
(5:18 –20). In between it treats the matter of seeking God and
seeking social good and what happens when the one is sought
without the other.

The doxology in Amos 5:8 –9 resembles closely the doxologies in 4:13 and 9:5 –6. It is possible that they are all parts of
a single hymn which Amos has quoted in his oracles. Since the
origin of such pieces was the ritual of the Israelite sanctuaries,
it is fitting that Amos used them to punctuate oracles concerning those very sanctuaries. The first occurs in an oracle sati-
rizing the cult of Bethel (4:4 –13). The second accompanies a
warning to the wise to avoid the cult places of Gilgal and
Bethel, lest they be destroyed with them (5:4 –6). The third is
part of the vision of God's destruction of the (unnamed) national sanctuary (9:1 –6).

These doxologies affirm God's power over all creation.
They are not primarily negative or threatening in their intent.
However, there is an ominous undertone in them, which be-
gins to emerge audibly in 5:8, and becomes quite clear in 9:5.
Together these brief hymnic pieces provide a thread which
ties the three oracles into a single sequence, mounting toward
a climactic oracle of doom for the cultic establishment of
Israel.

Ordinarily in Israel, seeking God meant worshiping at a
sanctuary, just as it does today. To go into the presence of God
is above all to go to church. Certain sanctuaries can come to
occupy so central a place in life—because of their architectur-
al and esthetic qualities, or their associations with decisive
events in a person's or people's history, or the sheer habit of
religious usage—that worshipers can count upon experienc-
ing the presence of God in these places, and, at the same time,
doubt the equal availability of such experience elsewhere.

Amos' oracles call into question the understanding of God
implied in such behavior. "Religious experience" may be at-
tained regularly at the sanctuaries, but it may be irrelevant or
even antithetical to "seeking the Lord," as the prophets

viewed this seeking. For them, seeking God meant necessarily seeking righteousness and social justice (5:7, 11 – 12, 15). Religion which did not foster these was futile, and the symbol of its futility was the destruction of the sanctuaries (5:5 – 6). Thus, the end of such religion was death. On the other hand, the end of seeking God truly was life (5:4).

The point of Amos' admonition to "seek Yahweh and live" was not that seeking social justice would secure the nation against political misfortune or military disaster. He seemed sure that the Israelite kingdom was going to be destroyed. However, if the people sought justice it was possible that God would "be gracious" to the remnant which survived (5:15). The oracle does not explain what this meant. What is implied, however, is that a just community finds fulfillment and satisfaction in the quality of its social relationships, regardless of the material circumstances of its life. Righteous relationships are their own reward. To have them is to live. God is gracious to the just community, not in the sense that he rewards them for their justice with prosperity, but in the sense that he gives assurance to the just that they are living in harmony with his will. The unjust society may survive for a time, but life within such a society may not be worth living. To have "life" is to live justly.

In Amos 1 – 2 we encountered the view that God was Lord of all nations and not merely the tutelary deity of Israel. Here we discover the assertion that he is master of the universe (5:8 – 9). This doxological statement is matched by the others in 4:13 and 9:5 – 6. All three of these passages occur in contexts which refer to Israel's worship at the great sanctuaries of the kingdom (4:4 – 5; 5:5; 9:1). Several things might be inferred from this juxtaposition: the power of God is manifest in nature and not in the sacrificial system of Israel's worship; or, the force threatening to destroy Israel is not a mere worldly power, but the Lord of the universe, against whom Israel's liturgical exertions are ineffective.

These inferences are negative. However, there is also a positive inference to be drawn from this acknowledgement of God's universal power—his capacity to control the vast forces of nature and of history. It is that Israel will not be destitute, without recourse to God, if her cities and temples are ruined; for the power and mercy of God, his wisdom and his right-

eousness, are the preconditions of life everywhere. It was not
Amos' purpose to point out this implication of his oracles, but
it is there, nevertheless. Hosea, Jeremiah, and Second Isaiah
expounded the significance of this idea of God in ways that
Amos did not. We will see how Hosea did this in our discussion of Hos 14.

"Is not the day of the Lord darkness and not light, and
gloom with no brightness in it?" (5:20). The modern preacher
may be tempted to use this verse as the text for a "hell-fire and
damnation" sermon. The temptation should be avoided.
Amos' idea of the day of Yahweh is not the same as the Christian idea of a Last Judgment. One concerns the destruction of
a kingdom in history, the other concerns the end of all history.
Although the seeds of the later conception of a universal day of
judgment at the end of time may be seen in the prophetic idea
of the day of Yahweh, the two should not be confused.

As far as the relevance of these two ideas to our life in the
twentieth century is concerned, the older prophetic preaching
contains a more useful social lesson, because it deals with the
actuality of history rather than a myth of "the world to
come." This myth can be given immediate relevance to the
lives of individual persons, as it is in most Christian preaching
on this theme, only by relating the eschatological judgment to
a supposed judgment of individuals after death. The moral
significance of the idea, then, is to elicit individual conver-
sions from unbelief to faith, and from sin to righteousness, in
order to avoid punishment after death. On the other hand, the
prophetic notion of the day of Yahweh is concerned first of all
with social and political institutions, with governments,
churches, economic and legal systems, business corporations,
trade unions, school systems, banks, medical and manufac-
turing associations, political parties, fraternal organizations,
welfare agencies, and military groups. It provides a perennial
warning of the precarious status and finite duration of all
such institutions, and a constant invitation to orient them in
ways which are socially constructive and not merely self-serving. It serves as a reminder that these are means and not ends,
worthy of only limited trust and allegiance; poor gods.

Meetings with God are full of surprises! When they happen we frequently find that the god we expected was an idol, a
projection of our own wishes and allegiances. The true God

disappoints these expectations, both in the present age and in
the "age to come," that is, the eschatological kingdom of his
righteousness. But, once we have surrendered our idols we
find deeper satisfaction than we dreamed of, in relation to the
source and goal of life. The life God gives us, at last, is better
and more enduring than what we had sought.

Piety Versus Social Action (5:21 –25)

Every reader of the Bible knows this famous text from
Amos. It is surely the best-known passage in the book: "I
hate, I despise your feasts. . . . But let justice roll down like
waters, and righteousness like an ever-flowing stream" (5:21
and 24). This strikes the contrast between religious ritual
and social justice about as sharply as it can be done. It also
sets forth the two sides of the debate over evangelical piety
and social action which is so lively in contemporary American Christianity.

Let's look first at what Amos said to Israel. It has often
been asserted that the prophets did not condemn religious ritual per se but only a ritualism which was unaccompanied by
zeal for social justice. There is a measure of truth in this assertion. However, the danger in it is that it tends to obscure a
number of distinctions which should be drawn concerning the
content and meaning of ritual. Worship takes many forms and
has many purposes, and it is important to take account of this
variety, and not merely talk about "ritual," as if it were uni-
form and constant.

The oracles of the preexilic prophets which deal most directly with Israel's worship are extremely harsh (e.g., Amos
5:21 –24; Hos 6:5 –6; 8:11 –13; and Isa 1:10 –17). There are no
explicit affirmations among them of a purified worship or of
worship which is matched by justice. It is an assumption of
modern commentators that the prophets objected to Israel's
worship only because it was tainted with baalism or because
of the lack of justice in the society. I do not wish to argue that
the prophets rejected all kinds of religious ritual as unaccept-
able to God, for there are no statements in the prophetic books
to justify this claim either. However, their criticism of ritual is
so sweeping and sustained that it seems fair to characterize it
as permanent skepticism. Not total rejection, but perennial
doubt. A staunch "show me" attitude.

We do not need to soften this prophetic opinion. There is ample warrant elsewhere in the Bible for our practice of public worship, so we should not feel compelled to make supporters out of the prophetic critics. On the contrary, we need them precisely as critics. All the temptations that beset Israel in her worship beset us, too: self-centeredness, self-indulgence, sentimentalism, sensualism, materialism, even superstition and, occasionally, magic. The prophets can help us keep our religious practices under scrutiny. If we care about the propriety and authenticity of our worship, in the light of the biblical witness, then we need the prophets.

It would be easy to avoid the prophets' blows if they were aimed only at animal-sacrifice and idolatry, as has often been thought. However, the entire range of liturgical acts comes under their attack. Here in Amos 5, singing and instrumental music are mentioned (5:23), and Isaiah even referred to prayer (Isa 1:15). Nothing we do in worship is immune to corruption. The question is always one of motive and purpose. Worship which fosters the love of neighbor, and all that this love implies, conforms to the biblical standard. Worship which undercuts such love, regardless of its form, deserves prophetic judgment.

Is corporate worship necessary for the people of God? The question asked in Amos 5:25 suggests that there was a time in Israel's history when she served God without resort to a sacrificial system (cf. Jer 7:22), and, although a system of public worship based upon animal sacrifice is not the only possible kind, Amos' question can serve by extension to raise the more general question of the necessity of worship, which is pertinent to our own religious situation. It seems to me that the answer to the general question is, Yes. Individuals may live righteous and faithful lives without participating regularly in public worship, but any community which desires to belong to "the Israel of God"—the people of the covenant—must worship God together. Despite Amos' disclaimer concerning the practice of sacrifice by Israel in the era of the wilderness wandering, there was never a time in Israel's life, as far as we know, when the people did not worship God in some regular, corporate fashion. The specific forms and content of worship varied according to time, place and circumstance, and some radical changes occurred over the long course of Israel's history. However, Israel—and the Apostolic church—never ceased to worship.

To summarize: the prophets were critical of Israel's worship because it tended to deteriorate into selfish, superstitious ritualism, which was unmatched by concern for social justice. Worship in our own religious communities is also susceptible to such ritualism. Nevertheless, corporate worship is indispensable to the people of God. The Church cannot be the Church without it. We can seek to purify our worship of all forms of "baalism" but we cannot do without it. On the other hand, as participants in the ritual life of the people of the covenant we are equally obligated to seek justice in our many communities.

Ritual piety and social action are both essential ingredients of the Christian life. Amos set the two over against each other in his famous oracle: "I hate ... your solemn assemblies. . . . But let justice roll down like waters!" This was a rhetorical exaggeration. We cannot follow its implication literally. In order to maintain our identity as the people of God we must worship God together. We must meet in "solemn assemblies." At the same time, we must pursue justice and righteousness in every dimension of our corporate existence. Not to do this is to worship some other god than the God of the prophets and the Apostles.

Amos 5:21 –25 contains a message for the church in every age, and it lends itself readily to preaching. The first point would be that worship without social action is not an adequate expression of biblical faith. The second would be that social action without worship cannot keep the church in being. Furthermore, the ground of worship and social action is the understanding of human beings as both spiritual and material children of God. According to the biblical witness, God is creator and redeemer of persons in community. The inward and outward dimensions of our lives are equally important, and they are inseparable. As faithful members of God's covenant community we care about the spiritual and material wellbeing of all of God's children and not merely about our own good.

Power and Pride (6:1 –14)

There are "those at ease in Zion" in every society. No political or economic system distributes power, wealth, and privilege fairly. Some systems do better than others, but none is ever completely just.

It is not the responsibility of the church as such to design or engineer political and economic systems. This is the responsibility of government and the citizens from whom government derives its authority. The responsibility of the church is to evaluate these systems in the light of the covenantal ethic of the Bible and the faith in God which undergirds it. The prophets of the OT did not propose new forms of government or socio-economic systems (except the writer of Ezekiel 40–48, who drafted a highly idealized scheme for a theocratic Israelite state governed by priests!). Amos and the other pre-exilic prophets attacked the social and economic injustices they saw in Israel but suggested no alternative structures. They should not be faulted for this. It would be naive to suppose they could have done more. The processes and structures of life in a large society are too complex and too durable for any individual or group within that society to change them. Nevertheless, for a prophet to keep silent in the face of problems which he discerns in the life of the community is to deprive it of insights that might help to ameliorate the evil. It is short-sighted to demand that critics keep quiet unless they propose alternatives.

Of course, many of the prophets' strictures were directed at the evil acts of individuals rather than evils inherent in the social system itself. Thus, corrupting a judicial procedure by accepting a bribe (5:12) can happen even in a good system. The antidote to such behavior is not the transformation of the system but the reform of the perpetrators.

Amos 6:1–14 deals with a situation which transcended the good or evil decisions of individuals. It was a problem of social class. A wealthy few ruled the nation and benefited in every way from the absolute monarchy which ruled it. In this passage Amos does not mention oppression of the poor or the other overt evils which are cited elsewhere in the book. The concern here is with an attitude, a disposition of the heart, a state of mind. It is pride, arrogance, and self-indulgence. It is languishing in luxurious ease and caring little about the wellbeing of the people as a whole (6:6). Feeling secure in their privileged position, the leaders of Israel pay no heed to the tale of history, a tale of ephemeral kingdoms and lost fortunes (6:2). Their chief concern is their own pleasure, and they are oblivious to the ominous course of national affairs.

Amos does not restrict these oracles to the royal court of Israel. Instead, he addresses the entire privileged class. Thus, his warning of the consequences of such behavior has a relevance beyond the limits of a monarchial state. It is a word which persons in power in any society might well ponder.

Ancient Israel was an agrarian and pastoral people, unlike ourselves, and the ways and means that elevated some to wealth and power differed in many respects from those that operate in our society. But Amos was not concerned with the social and economic processes which produced the evils he observed. He was concerned with the attitudes and behavior of those at the top. Therefore, his words are as timely today as they were in his own generation.

Amos prophesied that the arrogant, self-indulgent rich of Israel would be the first to go into exile when the nation fell (6:7). In this he was correct. Israel was a small nation. Its territory was approximately fifty miles wide and eighty miles long and its population probably no more than several hundred thousand. Under assault from a major foreign power, the upper class was terribly exposed, with nowhere to hide. Although they might not be the first to die in the fighting, they would be the first to be deported, under the policy established by the Assyrian kings in the eighth century B.C. Therefore, Amos' warning to them was borne out by the course of history.

The causal relationship between act and consequence is not so easy to trace in a huge, complex, technocratic society like ours. Modern preachers dare not threaten their congregations with specific punishments for their attitudes and behavior, in the manner of Amos. They would soon be embarrassed by the actual course of events. However, they can reflect on the uses and abuses of privilege. Not in Amos' words, to be sure! Amos' words are sharp, abrasive, sarcastic. Most modern listeners would be "turned off" by them, and thus miss their whole intention. The unprivileged, poor, and powerless might listen with relish, but the lesson might be wasted on them, and their own pride inflated instead. Better for the modern preacher to find less inflammatory ways of dealing with the issues.

This text is one to be preached to people who enjoy special privilege, not to the afflicted or deprived. The main message is that everyone suffers in the decline or death of a society. Wealth and power cannot provide refuge for the few. Their lives are bound up inextricably with those of the many. If this is true of communal calamity it is also true of communal prosperity. In the long run the good of each individual or segment of society is inseparable from the good of the people as a whole. Therefore, it makes good, practical sense to be concerned with the welfare of all. But, even more than this, it is right in God's eyes to do so.

Vision and Inspiration (7:1 – 9; 8:1 – 3)

Inspiration comes in many ways, to the prophet as well as the artist. The finished product of their skill usually requires the disciplined application of their best mental powers. However, a significant idea may come in a semi-conscious state—a dream or vision—and form the basis of a work of art or prophetic oracle. The human mind is always active, awake or asleep, and it is often in sleep that it organizes or responds to experience in a decisive or suggestive way. The images in a dream or vision may seem confused and irrational but they generally represent, often in symbolic form, the actuality of recent or remembered experience. One may relive in a dream something that has happened awake, and sometimes a dream will reflect aspects of experience which were perceived only subliminally while awake, and which thus went unnoticed. Furthermore, dreams are filled with feeling. Their emotional content is a remarkable index of important feelings in one's waking life, especially if these feelings have been obscured by the continuous barrage of sensory data or inhibited by the rational will. Thus, a dream may penetrate to what is most important in a person's inner experience or perception of reality.

Dreams and visions are not means by which new information about the world is received. The stuff of which dreams are made is provided by the waking mind and the senses. The subconscious mind works with the material provided by the conscious mind. Furthermore, the conscious mind must interpret a dream or vision in order for it to make sense. Therefore, dreams may provide telling clues to important aspects of human experience, but they are not a primary medium for acquiring knowledge.

Dreams and visions have been regarded widely in the history of human culture as means of revelation from the world of the gods. It is not surprising that this should be so, because they can be strange and powerful, uncanny and "supernatural." However, in the light of what we know about dreams today, we cannot regard them in the same way the ancients did. Images and ideas formed in the dreaming mind are no more significant in themselves than any others. They, too, exhibit the perceptions, attitudes and feelings of the dreamer, and they are subject to the same tests of meaning and validity as the images and ideas that fill the waking mind.

The prophets of Israel dreamed dreams and saw visions. The best known of these are the visions of Amos, which we are considering here, and those of Isaiah (Isa 6) and Ezekiel (Ezek 1–3; 8–11). Like most dreams they are filled with interesting symbols, and their emotional intensity and dramatic tension make them vivid and memorable. We have no way of knowing whether they were recalled just as they occurred or were recast in the process of recording. We can only take them as they come to us in their final, literary form. That they originated as dreams or visions testifies to the depth of conviction with which they were held by those who experienced them. However, the message they convey is no more, though no less, valid than that of the other prophetic writings.

Incidentally, exactly the same thing must be said about charismatic experiences, which have become popular again in some religious circles in our time. They are no more "spiritual," or "religious," or "true," or "meaningful" than other kinds of experience. Their level of feeling is high, but their significance as Christian experiences must be measured by their social context and their ethical consequences. If they contribute to love of the neighbor, with all this implies, they have positive value, according to the norm of the gospel. If they do not, especially if they foster sectarian pride, they actually thwart the work of the Holy Spirit, in whose name they are ostensibly cultivated.

Amos 7:1–9 and 8:1–3 form a single, unified narrative of a great visionary dialogue between the prophet and God, set against a series of four symbolic scenes. This unity has been disturbed somewhat by the insertion of 7:10–17, which recounts Amos' encounter with the priest Amaziah at Bethel.

The similarity between the prophecies of doom in this account (7:11 and 17b) and the one in the third scene of the vision (7:9b) may have led the editor to fuse the two passages together.

On the other hand, one might regard the entire section, 7:1 – 8:3, as a unity in its present form, with the first three scenes of the vision-narrative leading up to the dialogue with Amaziah, and the final visionary scene capping the whole, by repeating the divine word of doom.

If one has studied any of the earlier oracles in the book of Amos, it will come as no surprise to learn that the vision-narrative ends by prophesying the destruction of the Kingdom of Israel. However, one should not overlook other important dimensions of this text. Chief among them is the presentation of God as compassionate and long-suffering toward his people.

Many Christian readers, who may not know any better, and some Christian ministers, who ought to know better, think of "the God of the OT" as a God of justice—meaning wrath—and "the God of the NT" as a God of love. There are genuine differences between the message of the OT and that of the NT, but this is not one of them. The justice, or righteousness, of God is as much a concern of the NT as of the OT, and the love of God is as important in the OT as in the NT.

One of the sources of confusion in this matter is the failure to distinguish the various terms of the discussion, from text to text. For example, what an eighth-century B.C. prophet said about the destruction of a national state should not be compared simply with what the apostle Paul said about the forgiveness of an individual. One should always try to determine who or what the biblical writing is talking about, in what circumstances and to what ultimate ends, before drawing any broad theological conclusions from it.

Amos 7:1 – 6 not only represents God as patient and forgiving of Israel, but it also shows Amos as sympathetic toward his people. (Though his oracles concerned first of all the northern Israelite kingdom, he sometimes spoke about Israelites and Judeans together, as in 6:1, and, in referring here to "Jacob," seems to have meant the whole people of the covenant.) He was not a bitter outsider but a compassionate participant in the life of Israel. His wrath could be kindled by cruel, unjust acts, but this is evidence of moral sensitivity, not of callousness. To characterize Amos as a prophet of justice and Hosea as a prophet of love, as is often done, is unfair to both.

"The Lord repented" (7:3 and 6). What are we to make of this bold assertion? We soften it some if we translate it "relented" (NEB, JB, NJV), but the words still mean to change one's mind (TEV). How is it possible to say this about God?

The biblical writers used many anthropomorphic (and anthropopathic) similes and metaphors to talk about the disposition and deeds of God. We can only speak of God in the categories we know from our experience and our observation of the world. Our language only hints at the reality of God, whose being transcends our comprehension. However, the inadequacy of language is as true of the static categories of classical religious philosophy ("omnipotence," "omniscience," "impassibility") as it is of the dynamic categories of biblical faith. There is value in both. Naturally, the biblical metaphors should not be taken literally. This would reduce God to our own dimensions. However, these metaphors are necessary to maintain an adequate understanding of the freedom of God and his living relationship to his creatures. To say that God can "change his mind" is a perfectly good way of stressing the openness of life to new possibilities, and, on reflection, it surely seems less limiting than saying God cannot change. Change is more evident in the world than unchangeableness, and, if the world is grounded in the power and wisdom of God, then it is reasonable to think of God also as having the capacity to change. "His mind" is a metaphor, to be sure; but what could we say instead that would not be even more limiting?

Because Amos' report of his call to prophecy (7:14–15) has been placed next to the account of his great vision (7:1–9; 8:1–3), the latter has sometimes been regarded as an inaugural vision. It is possible that it functioned as his call to prophecy, though the text does not actually say it did; and it makes excellent sense as a vision of Israel's destruction, regardless of the time in the prophet's career when it occurred.

Calls to prophecy, like calls to the Christian ministry, are sometimes accompanied by vivid inward experiences, like a vision or audition, which can be described concretely and dated. The best example of such a call in the OT is Isaiah's (Isa 6),

and, in the NT, Paul's (Gal 1:11– 16; Acts 9:1– 9). Persons in
the church today who have "received" such a call to ministry
may derive great strength and sense of direction from it, while
those who have not, but are nevertheless interested in a professional career in the ministry, may worry about the depth
and certainty of their calling.

Concrete, datable calls to prophecy or ministry are products of the mind, like all dreams or visions. Some persons who
are genuinely called have them, and some do not. The validity
of the calling does not depend upon the form of the experience, but upon the interests, abilities, and sincerity of the person who has it. Intelligence, dedication, and discipline make a
true minister, and not a vivid conversion or call experience.
Christian vocation is grounded in faith and measured by faithfulness, and it is unimportant whether one ever has an experience like Isaiah's or Paul's. Amos reported a vision of Israel's
impending doom but said nothing about its being part of his
call to prophecy (7:15). Jeremiah did present his inaugural
commission in the form of a dialogue with God (Jer 1:4– 10),
with a visionary element (v.9); and Ezekiel's commission was
overwhelmingly visionary (Ezek 1– 3); but Hosea, Micah, Ha-
bakkuk and Zephaniah said nothing about similar experiences in their own lives.

To say that a vivid, or visionary, call to ministry is a product of the mind, as I have done, is not to invalidate it. It may
be a fully appropriate indication of the proper course of a person's life, and in this sense it may be taken to represent a call
from God, or a sign of God's will. Nevertheless, it is no more
"received" from God than any other inward experience. A quiet, gradually emerging sense of commitment to ministry—or
other form of religious dedication—is as much the work of
God as a loud, exploding one. Both are products of the cease-
less working of the mind and heart, conditioned by myriad in-
fluences from without, and by the decisions, attitudes, and
emotions of a lifetime.

Of course, an ancient call to prophecy was not identical to
a modern call to ministry. Prophecy was apparently not a professional career for the canonical, literary prophets of the OT,
and their prophetic activity was sometimes brief, in response
to a momentary historical situation. Their decisions to prophesy might therefore have been more impulsive and less life-

shaping than those of ministers of the church. Nevertheless, the responsibility of a prophet in ancient Israel was enough like that of the minister of the gospel in our time to justify our reflection on the prophet's experience as one clue to the meaning of Christian vocation in the modern church.

The episodes of Amos' vision move dramatically toward one end, pronouncement of destruction for the Kingdom of Israel under Jeroboam II. The sole concern of his dialogue with God (which takes place entirely within the vision) is whether or not this is going to happen. Twice God turns back from it, in response to Amos' appeal for compassion upon the smallness of "Jacob" (7:2 – 3, 5 – 6). Finally, however, the time for forbearance is exhausted and the judgment must be carried out (7:8 – 9). It is not explained why God eventually lost patience. Was it because of Israel's failure to respond to God's mercy with righteous behavior? Nothing at all is said about Israel's behavior throughout the course of the vision, before or after the decisions of God. All attention is focused on God's action. Therefore, we must turn elsewhere for a context for the vision.

It seems fair to explain the judgment itself as a punishment for social injustice, on the basis of Amos' oracles elsewhere in the book. His depiction of God's forbearance corresponds to the litany in 4:4 – 13, in which he refers to a series of past opportunities for reform which Israel has ignored, to her eventual destruction. Thus, the vision is a kind of parable of the history of Israel's relationship to God. Its message is that the time for reformation has run out. Opportunities existed, in the mercy of God, but they are exhausted. Only one outcome is possible now.

As a literary composition, Amos 7:1 – 9; 8:1 – 3 ranks with the remarkable opening oracle concerning the nations (1:2 – 2:16). It is such a finely crafted piece that it cannot be taken merely as the spontaneous recollection of a dream or vision. It exhibits the conscious artistry of a master writer. Since it is so well fashioned as a single whole, its effect would be enhanced when it was read in a service of worship today if it were read entire and not cut up into pieces. At the least, 7:1 – 9 should be read together. The fourth episode (8:1 – 3) repeats essentially what is said in the third (7:7 – 9), but the dramatic impact of the narrative as a whole is heightened if the fourth is included.

On the other hand, 8:1 –3 would have little dramatic effect if it
were read alone. The third and fourth episodes require the
first two for their rhetorical effect. There is a crescendo here
which is spoiled if the first two parts are omitted.

There is no need to explain all the individual details of the
vision when it is used as a scripture lesson in public worship.
It is not an allegory, in which each element symbolizes something in the real world. It is more like a parable, in which one
or two points are being made graphically. Devastation is
threatened (the locusts), but it is averted when the prophet intercedes and God relents. Once more, devastation is
threatened (fire), but the prophet intercedes again, and God
relents a second time. A third scene materializes in the mind's
eye (the plumb line), but this time God declares an end to his
forbearance and proclaims imminent disaster. And then once
more, a fourth time, a symbol of destruction takes shape (the
basket of fruit), and again, unmistakably, the sentence of
doom is pronounced. Such economy of phrasing, symmetry of
form, and boldness of imagery! All in all, this is a powerful
oracular statement.

How should one preach from this remarkable passage?
We have already mentioned the issue of vision and inspiration. This is one appropriate topic. The question of the feedom
and changelessness of God is another. A third is that of divine
forbearance and divine judgment. Another is the matter of
prophetic, or ministerial, intercession, or the role of media-
tion in the religious life.

Perhaps the hardest feature of the visions of Amos to
adapt to a modern sermon is their concrete imagery. It may be
best not to try to model a sermon on the dialogue of Amos and
God, or to seek parallels to the specific pictorial details in the
religious situation of a modern congregation. The results
might be artificial and histrionic. However, the narrative itself reads well as a dramatic prologue to the topical issues
suggested above.

Confrontation in Bethel (7:10 –17)

Nothing in our religious practice, or our culture, quite
corresponds to an oracular pronouncement by a prophet of
God in ancient Israel. Within our religious communities the
roles of priest, rabbi, and minister are much broader in scope

and more pastoral. Many preachers feel obligated to include a
prophetic element in their message, but it is only one part of
the faith they must proclaim. Outside religion there are many
prophetic voices, that is, critics of government, business, society, or culture, but they do not speak from an explicit theological viewpoint and they do not address a community which
understands itself as the people of God. Perhaps even more
important than these differences between Amos' situation and
ours is the change which has taken place since biblical times
in people's understanding of the power of words.

In the world of ancient Israel religious utterances were
taken with utmost seriousness. Blessings and curses, oaths,
priestly judgments, benedictions, vows, prayers and oracles
were invested with a power that we seldom if ever attribute
to words alone. It is not surprising then that Amos was regarded as a dangerous man by the Israelite authorities just
because he published oracles of judgment concerning the
nation. The priest Amaziah, who was probably the chief
priest of the central sanctuary in Bethel, called his speaking
a conspiracy (7:10)!

There are analogies to this event in some countries of the
world today. Totalitarian states of the right and left prohibit
free speech and punish critics as criminals. In non-totalitari-
an nations like our own, however, where freedom of speech
and the press are supported, an incident like the one in Bethel
could hardly occur. Not only would Amos' right to speak be
protected, but his speaking would not be regarded as dangerous. Since everyone is free to speak and publish, words are everywhere, continually, and no word can have much impact.
Speech is free and words are cheap. So it requires an effort of
imagination to put ourselves in Amaziah's place and realize
what all the fuss was about.

We must remember, too, that religion was not a separate
aspect of life. It permeated all the institutions of society. Nation and church were one. Kingship was sacred. The power
and will of God were thought to be manifest in all dimensions
of life. Therefore, when a man like Amos spoke against the
leadership of the nation, the judicial system, the economic
practices, or the temple, he undermined society as a whole. So
the leaders tried to get rid of him. As far as we know, Amos
was not martyred. He was merely expelled from Israel—sent
back to Judah where he had come from.

We have said that prophets are not treated as criminals in our society and that their words are more likely to go unnoticed amid the endless cacophony of voices around us than to be taken as a cause for alarm. However, modern ministers who are faithful to the full scope of the biblical message in their preaching and teaching can expect to alienate some members of their congregations, at least some of the time. Injustice, cruelty, oppression, dishonesty, greed, sloth, pride, and selfishness abound in our society as they did in ancient Israel. Most church people are not as blatantly involved in evil as those whom Amos criticized, so it takes greater subtlety and discretion on the preacher's part to deal with these issues effectively. Furthermore, we know more fully than Amos ever imagined the extent to which social evils are inherent in the very structures and processes of corporate life. "Systemic evil" we call it today. By whatever name, it is real and ever present. Silence in the face of the difficulty and complexity of the problems serves only to compound the evil. It is better for the preacher to risk oversimplification than to say nothing about these issues. No one person has the last word. The prophetic preacher is not supposed to bring the dialogue to an end, but to get it started and to keep it going.

In the previous section we discussed calls to prophecy in relation to visions. Here we must discuss the call of Amos as he described it in his reply to Amaziah (7:14–15).

Two issues arise in this confrontation between Amos and the priest Amaziah. Was Amos formally a prophet or was he a "layman"? If he was a prophet, was he a professional? Modern discussion of these questions has not been entirely neutral. At times it has been colored by anticlericalism and antiprofessionalism, especially among Protestant commentators. The zeal to deny any connection on Amos' part with priestly or prophetic circles has sometimes cloaked these biases. The assumption which lies behind this view is that an "unspoiled" layman, called "directly" by God to ministry, is more trustworthy than a minister who is selected and trained through an institutionalized process.

As far as possible it is well to keep our exegesis of the biblical text uncluttered by our view of ministry in the church today. For those who demand it, there is ample biblical warrant for any one of several conceptions of ministry. Therefore, one need not be anxious to show that that all the important bibli-

cal texts support one's own view (unless of course one believes
in the uniformity and inerrancy of the biblical witness). Better
to let the text speak for itself. Once we have heard it we can
judge whether the questions it raises are our questions and
whether it helps us to answer our questions in ways that are
meaningful for our own situation.

It seems to me that the central point of Amos' confrontation with Amaziah was whether he should prophesy in Bethel,
and not whether he was a prophet or seer, a layman or a professional. Amaziah's injunction to him reaches its climax with
the statement, "Never again prophesy at Bethel" (7:13).
Amos' reply is, "You say, 'Do not prophesy against Israel,' but
God sent me, saying, 'Go, prophesy to my people Israel'"
(7:16, 15). Although this puts the statements of God and
Amaziah in the reverse order in which they occur in the text, it
seems to me to convey the main point he was making. The
question then was Who had the authority to determine where
and when a person could prophesy in the name of God? Was it
the prophet himself or the political and ecclesiastical leaders?
It was not a choice between God's authority and the leaders',
for although Amos said that God had sent him, this was just as
much a human opinion as Amaziah's probable conviction that
he himself was the ordained representative of God.

Whether or not Amos claimed the formal status of prophet—or, in Amaziah's word, seer—is incidental to the account
of his call. He simply said that he had been a shepherd, and
not a prophet, when God sent him to prophesy. Any allusion to
professionalism here is secondary, whether it be Amaziah's
sarcastic dismissal of Amos or our debate about the exact nu-
ances of the dialogue between the two men. Apparently Amos
was a non-professional prophet. Indeed, it is possible that he
did not regard himself as a prophet at all, in any formal sense
of the word. And yet he composed and delivered masterly oracles on the life and destiny of Israel, and exercised a major influence upon the subsequent course of religious thought. His
background, training, and status were unimportant. Only his
oracles mattered.

Prophetic voices like Amos' can emerge at any time.
When they do, we can only be grateful for their contribution
to religion and the cause of justice. However, the church cannot depend upon such figures for its ministry. They appear
spontaneously—and rarely. The church requires large num-

bers of trained, disciplined professional leaders if the vast, continuous work of ministry is to be done. These leaders perform only a small part of the church's total ministry. The rest is done by the laity. But the ministry of the laity in the church is not the same thing as the prophetic ministry performed by a man like Amos. That was a special vocation, for which he had a special gift. Amos cannot serve as the ordinary model for lay ministers in our religious communities.

Amos 7:17 is a savage condemnation of Amaziah and his family. What can we make of a word like this in our effort to appropriate the scriptures? It sounds so much like the vindictive attack of an ostracized prophet. Is it nothing more than hateful spite?

We probably should not try to soften the sharp edges of this prophecy, or deny that there was a measure of vengefulness in Amos' mind when he made it. Nor does it help to say that his indignation was not caused by a personal slight but a slight to the word of God. By this kind of rationalization we can justify almost anything in the name of religion! Merely believing that one is speaking for God does not make it so, nor does it excuse one's excessive behavior.

Having said this, though, we should add that Amos' prophecy of the fate of Amaziah was a logical extension of his belief that the end was coming for Israel. The leaders of the nation would be the first to fall, or be deported, when the nation was conquered, as Amos believed it would be. So, in this sense, Amos' word about Amaziah was not a personal attack. It was a corollary of his larger proclamation of doom.

There are several themes in Amos 7:10–17 which are important for the witness of the church today. One is our obligation to speak prophetically on matters of social justice and public morality, despite the possible cost. Another is the challenge to the laity of the churches to share in the ministry of the gospel which is properly theirs. Yet another is the responsibility of the church to criticize itself in the light of the gospel. Finally, we may note the theme of confidence in the power of the preached word to judge and to redeem.

The End of a Nation (8:4–14; 9:1–6)

"Listen here, all of you who exploit the poor and oppress the weak. . .!"

If a preacher today began a sermon this way, would anyone listen? None of us would think it was meant for us, for we would not recognize ourselves as oppressors. Was it different for Amos' audience? Did he expect anyone to pay attention? Were they more tolerant than we? Judging by Amaziah's response to Amos' preaching (7:10–13), this seems unlikely. Probably Amos' oracles were paid little heed until after his prophecy of the fall of Israel had been fulfilled. We know nothing about the history of his writings except that they found their way ultimately into the prophetic canon. However, on the basis of allusions to the preservation of the oracles of Isaiah (Isa 8:16–20) and Jeremiah (Jer 36), we may assume that they were recorded and transmitted by a few persons close to the prophet. They were preserved, against the day when the word of God would be vindicated and they would elicit a constructive response. The vitality of words like Amos' is not exhausted in their author's lifetime. They survive, to goad, to challenge, to instruct, from generation to generation. Thus, their worth is not measured by the initial reaction of their audience.

The section we are considering contains two major units, 8:4–14 and 9:1–6, each of which is composed of several smaller pieces (8:4–8; 8:9–10; 8:11–12; 8:13–14; 9:1–4; 9:5–6). There is too much here to be used for a single scripture lesson or sermon. However, the sayings may be studied together and when this is done, they have a powerful impact. Like all poetry this material should be read aloud, and not too rapidly. The section begins with one of the fuller charges of social injustice in the book (8:4–6), and continues with several vivid pictures of the end of Israel (8:7–9:4). It concludes with a hymnic apostrophe to the grandeur and power of God (9:5–6), which gives weight to the oracles delivered in his name.

Amos may have been a shepherd, but he was also a master poet. His oracles are varied, inventive, finely constructed, vivid, and memorable. We know nothing about his tutelage or the manner of his literary working. We can only celebrate his gift.

Many of the motifs contained in these poems have been presented in other forms elsewhere in the book, but there are several new ideas which merit special attention.

"The Lord has sworn by the pride of Jacob: 'Surely I will never forget any of their deeds' " (8:7). Was Amos right? Does

God have an indelible memory of everyone's deeds? This is a very sobering thought. The point Amos was making here was that the oppressors in Israel would not get away with their evil deeds in the long run. They might prosper for a time, but eventually the justice of God would overtake them and they would suffer the punishment they deserved. This conviction is expressed frequently in the Bible, notably in the psalms (e.g., Ps 73) and the speeches of the friends of Job (e.g., Job 20). It has also played an important part in religious thought down to the present time.

The OT writers who held this belief were convinced that God's justice would be effected within the actual lifetime of persons, for they did not believe in an afterlife. However, as time went on, it became evident from observation of the actual course of human affairs that evil deeds often went unpunished. Injustice and oppression could persist for generations and the oppressors enjoy happier lives than the "righteous poor" whom they oppressed. For this and other reasons the doctrine of an afterlife took shape in Judaism. Many ideas were associated with it, but one of the most important was that of an eschatological judgment, in which all people would receive reward or punishment for their lifetime's deeds. This belief is still prominent among religious people today. It is the principal assumption underlying the appeal for conversion in the vast world of television evangelism and other forms of popular Christian crusade.

A brief exposition of the Book of Amos is not the place to discuss this question fully. There are far too many facets of it and far too many relevant biblical texts. All we can properly do is to take note of Amos' belief in the indelible memory of God, and suggest some of the questions to which the belief gives rise.

Does God remember all our good deeds as well as all the evil ones? Is it really the concern of God to see that all human behavior is graded and rewarded? Is there in the providence of God no escape from the legacy of the past? Is there any genuine freedom to begin afresh, to chart a new course? What is the meaning of God's mercy in relation to his memory of our deeds? What does the love of God imply concerning our ultimate worth and meaning? Amos' words concerned the Kingdom of Israel and were not originally meant to apply to all people in all times. But if what he said was true of God's memory of Israel's life, must it not be true also of God's memory of ours? These are among the issues which this text poses for our concerted reflection.

" 'Behold, the days are coming,' says the Lord God, 'when I will send a famine . . . of hearing the words of the Lord. They shall wander from sea to sea. . . to seek the word of the Lord, but they shall not find it' " (8:11 – 12).

People live by words. We search for the right word to give meaning to a moment or a relationship. Ideas come into being through the medium of words. Persons are known by their speaking, the shape and sound and sense of their words. Cultures endure and are remembered by their distinctive words, learned and celebrated. To forget the words of a person or a culture is to lose that person or culture, in the sense that matters most. Israel's life was formed by the words of the fathers, the Mosaic tradition, the mediators of the covenant, the prophets—words informed by a vision of the nature and purpose of God, which made them the word of God. Without this word Israel could not continue to be Israel, for it was this word, and not kinship, or geography, or political organization, that defined her being. This word required continual repetition and celebration if Israel were not to forget who she was. It needed new interpreters in every generation, probing its depths, finding new dimensions of its meaning, testing Israel's life in the light of its demands. So when Amos warned about a coming famine of the word, he spoke about the loss of the center.

In our age the people of God are a vast company, a thousand times the number of ancient Israel. There is no danger that the survival of the word or its vitality would depend upon one or two or several—like Elijah, saying, "I, even I only, am left [of the prophets of the Lord]" (1 Kings 19:14). There are millions of prophets—preachers—interpreters of the word— using diverse media in a multitude of styles. And yet, the importance of the word to the people gathered in each place at any time is as great as ever. It is beyond reckoning.

We have suggested a number of topics which would be appropriate to consider when expounding these texts from Amos. One is the indelible memory of God, and another is the vitality of the word. Like all topics from the prophets, these can be developed in the light of the full witness of the Bible. God's memory of us is the principal ground of assurance of the meaning of our lives. Although this memory includes trage- dies and failures, it is biased in our favor. In the end, God loves us in spite of everything, and bestows eternal significance on everything good we have been and done and shared. Sanc- tuaries may fall (9:1 – 6) and preaching may cease (8:11 – 12), but God does not die in such times. He remains fully active amidst his people, waiting for the right moment and the right response to bring worship and word into creative being again.

A Distant Hope (9:11 – 15)

After the fall, what? As we shall see, Hosea had a lot to say about this, just a few years after Amos and in the same place. But Amos had nothing to say. This bright ending of the book is not his. There is not a single note in it of the great ethical themes which control his oracles, nor the least echo of his pas- sion for justice. These last lines of the book bespeak an entire- ly different situation in the life of Israel. They are rightly dated by most scholars in the postexilic period.

Amos' last word was devastating: "Not one of them shall escape!" (9:1). The slender hope he had had for a "remnant of Joseph," to whom God might be gracious (5:14 – 15), had giv- en way to despair over the entire Kingdom of Israel. There was perhaps a measure of rhetorical exaggeration in his insis- tence that God would ferret out every last one of the people for destruction, wherever they might hide, throughout the whole wide world (9:2 – 4). But even if we make an allowance for this hyperbole, there was nothing in Amos' own prophecy to build hope upon.

If we need a reason to explain the lack of hope in Amos' proclamation, one possibility lies in the timing of his minis- try. According to the evidence of the book, he prophesied only during the reign of Jeroboam II of Israel (1:1; 7:10 – 11). Jero- boam's reign ended about 746 B.C., or approximately 25 years before the fall of Samaria. Thus, Amos' whole career fell in a time of security and prosperity in Israel. None of the calami- ties he expected occurred while he was active as a prophet. Therefore, there was no reason for him to say anything about the aftermath of the fall. The only relevant word for him to speak was one of moral criticism and imminent danger. Consequently, we should not compare him invidiously with other prophets, whose careers spanned several historical situations, and whose message, as a result, was more varied.

Even if 9:11 –15 is not Amos', it is still part of the book as it comes to us, and it deserves our consideration. There were survivors of the fall of Samaria, although the Bible tells us little about them. Yahwism continued to be practiced in the subjugated kingdom, at least until the reign of Josiah, king of Judah (ca. 640 –609 B.C.), who obliterated the remnants of the cult in the north at the time of his religious reformation (621 B.C.; 2 Kings 23:15 –20). As far as we know, Judah was the bearer of Yahwistic tradition after this time. The end of the book of Amos reflects this fact, for it exhibits a Judean perspective. The concern for the restoration of the Davidic kingship (9:11) and the hostility toward the rival Kingdom of Edom (9:12) are typical postexilic Judean sentiments, neither of which had any place in Amos' own writing. However, the main thing we need to acknowledge as we try to appropriate the meaning of the book for the ongoing life of the people of God is not that the later Judean editors of the OT appended alien notions to the oracles of Amos, but that they preserved his oracles—presumably intact—and in their own way bore witness to the continuing work of God in their midst. The word of God was kept alive after all. Amos was wrong about this (9:12). Kingdoms could fall, cities crumble, and institutions fade away, but the prophetic tradition would live on through the ages, preserved and enlarged by an endless line of witnesses. Most of them, like the editor of the Book of Amos, remained anonymous; but their identity was not important. All that mattered was their witness to the word.

One of the themes of Amos 9:11 –15 has come into prominence in Judaism in the twentieth century. It is the promise of Israel's restoration in the land of her ancient settlement (9:14 –15). Most Jews and some Christians view the establishment of the state of Israel as the fulfillment of this, and related, OT prophecies. Others regard these prophecies as having to do only with the postexilic restoration of Jerusalem and Judea. One may well wonder whether the OT writers had any interest in events 2000 years after their time. Be that as it may, the basic issue raised by these verses is whether the people of God require particular places for their existence. No one can survive apart from land, but is there any special land, or lands, cities, monuments, temples, which are necessary for the fulfillment of God's covenant with Israel? Is it possible for pride of place and attachment to place to undermine obedience to God? When does possession of place become an end in itself, justifying moral compromise and undercutting the love of the neighbor? These are issues not only for modern Zionism, but for religious communities of all kinds and denominations to deal with. Furthermore, we do not wish to imply that places are unimportant. To a considerable extent, we are what we have experienced, and our life-shaping experiences often are bound up with particular places. We would be impoverished to lose the memory and meaning of these places. Nor should we disdain what is of the earth, earthy, in the name of "spiritual" values. According to biblical faith, the earth and its effects are truly good and beautiful, truly God's. Our life is indissolubly bound to it at every level of our being. Not merely to the world in general, but to the world in its particular parts, concretely. So there is a sense in which the writer of Amos 9 spoke for us all.

There are several ways to deal with the last chapter of the Book of Amos. One is to consider Amos' own final word concerning the Kingdom of Israel. Kingdoms really do fall and nations die. So do institutions of all sorts. The institutions we participate in and hold dear are finite, imperfect, and subject to eventual disappearance. We should not stake our happiness or the meaning of our lives upon them. This is a lesson to be learned from ancient Israel, as it was interpreted by the prophet Amos.

Another approach to the chapter is to listen to the message of the anonymous, postexilic editor who added the word of hope. In the providence of God there is no utterly hopeless situation. There is always a creative future for those who have faith. In this age of rapid and unsettling social change, the people of God have nothing ultimately to fear. Our future is not bound to our social institutions but to the creator of heaven and earth (9:5–6).

HOSEA

Introduction

So little is known about Hosea that we must regard him as an anonymous prophet. We know the names of his father, his wife, and three of his children, and the approximate time of his work (1:1 –8), but that is all. His words survive; his life story does not. Thus, like most of the writers of the OT, he is known simply as a spokesman of God, nothing more.

Much has been made of Hosea's marriage as a key to understanding the man and his message. A few facts about his marriage, or marriages, are given in chaps 1 and 3, but they actually tell us little about the man. His marriage to Gomer and that to the woman in chap 3 (who may have been Gomer also) are presented to us as symbolic actions conveying a prophetic message, and not primarily as acts in a personal relationship between husband and wife. Insofar as the acts mentioned in the text are concerned, this relationship appears to have been subordinated to the prophet's sense of responsibility to declare the word of God. Of course, the fact that a man would undertake a marriage, or two, for this purpose, and also burden his children with names which to our mind would be psychologically crippling, tells us something important about the man. Obviously, his prophetic vocation was the most important thing in his life. The subordination of one's private life to one's prophetic calling is a hallmark of the OT prophets and it is nowhere more manifest than here.

As far as Hosea's origins are concerned, we know nothing except his father's name (Beeri; 1:1). His ministry seems

to have been conducted entirely within the northern Kingdom of Israel. He frequently refers to this kingdom, or its
people, as Ephraim. This may indicate that he himself came
from the tribe of Ephraim, or the central hill country of what
later became known as the region of Samaria, which was the
traditional territory of the tribe of Ephraim. On the other
hand, he may have used this designation because Ephraim
was the most prominent component of the northern kingdom, in ancestry and location. There are a few references to
Judah in the book, but most of these appear to be editorial
notes added to the oracles at a later time. It must be
remembered that the OT writings came to us through Judean hands. The writings which originated in the northern
kingdom, or its antecedents, have been edited or supple-
mented at some points by Judean scribes. The references to
Judah in Hos 4–14 are judgmental (4:15; 5:5, 10, 12, 13, 14;
6:4, 11; 8:14; 10:11; 11:12; 12:2; Hos 11:12 should be translated, "Judah again strays with El, and is faithful to 'holy
ones.' "). None of these allusions affects our understanding
of Hosea's theology.

The references to Judah in chaps 1–3 are another matter.
Hos 1:7 is pro-Judean and the allusion in 3:5 is pro-Davidic.
The majority of commentators regard these as later Judean
additions to the original message of Hosea, a judgment with
which I agree. On the other hand, there are many who regard
the reference in 1:11 as original. Since it occurs in a promise of
the eventual reunification of all Israel, under their one God, it
expresses a hope that any prophet, Israelite or Judean, might
have held. This passage is indeed an important one theologically, and it must be taken account of in any full exposition of
the message of the book.

The editorial superscription to the book dates Hosea's
prophetic work in the reign of Jeroboam II of Israel (1:1). This
makes him a contemporary of Amos (Amos 1:1). However,
neither prophet mentions the other. Of course, Jeroboam's
reign lasted about 40 years, so they could easily have missed
each other; and even if one had been aware of the other, he
would not necessarily have mentioned him in his oracles.

In addition to the reference to Jeroboam, the editors of
the books have dated the two prophets according to the reigns
of the kings of Judah. Amos is placed in the reign of Uzziah

(Amos 1:1), while Hosea is placed in that of Uzziah and his three successors (Jotham, Ahaz and Hezekiah; Hos 1:1). Uzziah's reign ended about the same time as Jeroboam's, namely, 745–740 B.C., while the last reign mentioned in Hosea ended after 700 B.C. This dating probably extends Hosea's ministry much too far. However, if we take the chronological statement in Hos 1:1 in a more general sense, it seems to indicate that Hosea was known to have prophesied after the end of Jeroboam's reign, that is to say, in the time of troubles leading up to the destruction of the Kingdom of Israel in 721 B.C. As we shall see in the discussion of Hos 8, such a date also seems to be implied by some of the things Hosea himself said. Thus we may repeat what was said in the introduction to the book of Amos, namely, that Amos' work seems to have been done entirely before the era of Israel's collapse, while Hosea's extended into that era.

This difference in historical setting helps to account for a major difference in the content of the message of Amos and Hosea. The original oracles of Amos prophesy only doom for the Kingdom of Israel. They do not go beyond that doom to promise a new phase in the life of Israel after the fall. Such a promise, however, is a major element in the proclamation of Hosea. Rather than account for the differences in terms of the temperaments or theologies of the two prophets, I would prefer to explain the difference on the basis of their historical settings. If Amos prophesied entirely in an era of prosperity, it would not have made sense for him to talk about a future restoration after the fall of the existant kingdom. His concern would have been to call attention to current evils and warn of impending destruction. To talk about anything beyond that would have been irrelevant to the existential situation of his audience.

The situation of Hosea's audience would have been quite different. They would already have begun to experience the turmoil and anarchy which characterized the final decade of the kingdom and which led up to its fall. A promise of re-creation after destruction would have been entirely appropriate in that situation. Israel had already entered the era of wrath, and faith in the continuing power and righteousness of God would have entailed a prophetic word of hope in such circumstances.

The Book of Hosea, like the Book of Amos, is a somewhat haphazard collection of poetic oracles. The majority of these are oracles of judgment, but a number of them are promises of salvation beyond the judgment. At some points we can discern a conscious design in the editorial arrangement of the materials. There is a more evident plan in this case than in Amos'. The book falls into two parts, of unequal length. Chaps 1 –3 revolve around the marriage of Hosea to Gomer (chap 1) and his remarriage to her or to some other unnamed woman (chap 3). These marriages are represented as prophetic actions symbolic of the "marriage" of God to Israel. This metaphor of the covenant relationship dominates this first section of the book.

Hos 4 –14 does not exhibit any overall design, except that the final oracle reiterates the promise of re-creation which is an important component of Hosea's overarching theology of Israel's history. It makes a fitting conclusion to the collection of his oracles. The placement of the rest of the materials in the book seems to be arbitrary.

Our treatment of the book follows the chapter divisions of the printed Bible, for the most part. These divisions are reasonable ones, and they provide a convenient structure for our discussion. Nevertheless, many of the chapters concern more than one oracle, and all of these can be broken down into smaller poetic units. Where it seems necessary to do so, these sub-divisions will be noted. However, the reader should consult a commentary for a more detailed literary analysis.

Covenant as Marriage (1:1 –3:5)

The images which dominate Hosea's picture of God and Israel are drawn from the family: husband-wife and parent-child. Of all the metaphors used to speak about God, these two convey most successfully the combination of attributes essential to the biblical understanding of God's relationship to his people: intimacy, dependability, comprehensiveness, duration, and authority. Other metaphors convey one or more of these attributes, but not all of them. King, judge, warrior, savior, and physician are among the examples that can be cited.

The family metaphors appear less often in the OT as a whole than some others, especially the image of God as King; but their importance to us theologically is not measured by mere frequency of occurrence. Clearly, the idea of God as

Father came to be the central theme of the NT gospels; therefore, the OT writings which speak of God in this way have special significance for all Christian readers. Hos 11 is one of these. Similarly, the bridal metaphor, which controls Hos 1 – 3, recurs in the NT, as an image of the relationship of Christ to his church (Matt 9:14 – 15; John 3:29; Rev 22:17).

We have entitled this section "Covenant as Marriage," because Hosea's message is grounded explicitly in the covenantal tradition. This is not true of all the preexilic prophets. For example, Amos and Isaiah make little direct use of the Exodus-Sinai tradition. Whether or not this tradition undergirded their thought has been debated by biblical scholars. However, there is no question about its significance for Hosea. It dominates the book.

Like a parent, God loves his people, is patient, compassionate, and merciful toward them, values them for their own sake, suffers when they suffer, and desires their health and happiness. There is no limit to the range of his concern. It comprehends their whole life, everything. Nor is there any limit to the duration of his love. It lasts as long as they live. As sustainer of life, God is dependable and true. As guardian of the family's integrity, he is teacher, disciplinarian, and protector. He is their principal source of security and their moral arbiter. In all of these respects, the role of a human parent serves as an analogy to the being and activity of God.

In biblical times the husband-wife relationship served almost as well as that of parent-child as a metaphor of God's relationship to Israel, and it would still do so in some cultures today. However, in our society this is not the case. Husbands do not have authority over their wives, and wives are less and less dependent upon their husbands, as they gain equality with them. Therefore, since the people of God are not God's equals, but depend upon him for the very conditions of their life, the metaphor of marriage has lost much of its theological appropriateness in our time. One must remember this when expounding the message of Hosea to a modern audience. It is also true that the parent-child relationship has changed in recent generations. Nevertheless, it is still enough like that of biblical times to give this metaphor continued usefulness in our religious discourse.

Hos 1:1 –3:5 is rich material. Each of the three chapters should be used separately in preaching, but since they throw light upon each other they can usefully be treated together here. Chap 1 is a kind of prophetic tract, recounting four symbolic actions performed by Hosea as dramatic vehicles of his message. Chap 2 is a poetic history of God's covenant with Israel, using the metaphor of marriage as a narrative device. Chap 3 is the account of another symbolic action performed by the prophet. This and the four signs in chap 1 involve his wife or children and thus utilize his role as husband and father in close connection with his activity as a prophet.

The four signs described in chap 1 were enacted over a period of at least three years, since they involve the naming of three children born to Hosea and his wife Gomer. However, the chapter as it comes to us is a unified literary whole, carefully wrought and building to a climax, like the narrative of Amos' four visions (Amos 7:1 –9; 8:1 –3).

Under a sense of divine command, Hosea married a harlot to symbolize the relationship of God to a harlotrous people. Gomer may have been known publicly as a prostitute—sacred or profane—when Hosea married her, or her behavior may have developed only afterward and been made by him into the symbol of Israel's behavior. In either case, the cost to Hosea in personal suffering must have been enormous. It is characteristic of OT writers to understate the emotional reactions of the actors in a narrative—whether historical or fictional—so it is not surprising that nothing is said here about Hosea's feelings. However, with a moment's reflection we know what these would have been.

The symbolic marriage of Hosea and Gomer suggested the indictment of Israel: "married" to Yahweh through the covenant, she had become an unfaithful, whorish wife. The three remaining signs signalled the punishment to fall upon the wayward nation. All three were names given to the children of this strange marriage.

"Jezreel" (1:4 –5) was to be taken as a walking reminder of the punishment to fall upon the dynasty of Jehu—in whose line stood the reigning king Jeroboam II—for the slaughter of the house of Ahab, by which Jehu established his own rule (2 Kings 10:1 –14). "Not Pitied" (1:6) extended the pronouncement of doom to the whole Kingdom of Israel (1:7, sparing

Judah, is probably a secondary, Judean addition to the text).
"Not My People" (1:8 –9) declared the end of an era by nullify-
ing the covenantal relationship of Israel with Yahweh (there is
a play on Exod 3:12 –15 in v 9).

In the Hebrew Bible, chap 1 ends at this point and the following promise of restoration (1:10 –2:1 in the English Bible)
goes with chap 2. In this latter place it serves with 2:21 –23 as
a frame around the account of apostasy, chastisement, and
covenant-renewal in 2:2 –20. This seems to be the better division of literary units. In either case, of course, the reversal of
names in 1:1 –2:1 and 2:22 –23 presupposes the original naming of Hosea's children in 1:4 –9.

Hos 2 is an allegorical poem interpreting the whole covenantal history of Israel. The allegorical figure is a marriage,
with Israel as the bride of Yahweh. The poetic drama moves
through a full cycle of marriage, divorce, discipline, and remarriage. Thus it goes beyond covenant abrogation and national disaster to national reformation and covenant-renewal.
By prophesying the future era of a new covenant, Hosea distinguished himself from Amos, who dealt only with the ill-fat-
ed era of the old covenant. The grand design of Israel's
covenantal story—past, present, and future—which is declaimed so eloquently in chap 2, is symbolized compactly in
the dramatic act of chap 3, is restated again in the famous
poem about parent and child in chap 11, and underlies the
whole collection of Hosea's oracles.

There are three scenes in the allegorical drama. In the
first (2:2 –13) the husband pleads for the reform of his faithless wife. She is an adulteress, obsessed with the lovers who
lavish gifts upon her. The husband, of course, is Yahweh; the
wife, Israel; and the lovers, the gods of the Canaanite nature
religion. Adoring them because of their favors—grain, wine,
and oil—she is actually deluded, for it is Yahweh, not these
supposed gods, who is responsible for the fertility of the
earth. However, neither persuasion (2:2 –5) nor discipline
(2:6 –8) succeeds in breaking through her habits of mind and
action; therefore, sterner measures are required. She will be
forcibly taken from the land and made to live in the wilderness (2:9 –14).

The second scene takes place in the wilderness (2:15 –20).
Here at last the wife comes to her senses, regains the early de-

votion of her marriage, and becomes capable of entering into a renewed relationship of faithfulness and love.

In the final scene, the bride is given once more the good things of the earth (2:21 – 23), and she, and her children, now understand the true source of all blessings (v. 23).

This story of God and Israel was dramatized in the symbolic action performed by Hosea with his adulterous wife (chap 3). In spite of her infidelity, he rescued her from her dereliction. He continued to hope for her reformation of life, and he knew that serious discipline was necessary for this to come about. He promised her full status as his wife if she could learn fidelity, and he provided the restraints that would give her the opportunity to do so. Thus, the prophet enacted in his own domestic life the story of God's dealings with Israel. His act was not merely symbolical of the prophetic message he wished to proclaim, but was also an act of love toward his wife.

The literary design of Hos 1 – 3 is elegant. Compact narratives of Hosea's symbolic actions begin and end the section, providing a framework for the whole (1:2 – 9 and 3:1 – 5). Promises of Israel's future restoration, which are highlighted by the reversal of the symbolic names of 1:4 – 9, come immediately within this frame, in a chiastic arrangement (1:10 – 2:1 and 2:21 – 23). At the center stands the great allegorical poem on the story of Israel's marriage/covenant with God (2:2 – 20). All in all this is one of the masterpieces of prophetic literature.

The religious issue involved in these chapters is the conflict between devotion to Yahweh and devotion to the Canaanite nature-deities. This issue dominates the entire book of Hosea and yet seems so foreign to our religious concerns today, that we must ponder its significance carefully if we are to make any serious use of Hosea's oracles in our own situation.

Canaanite Baalism deified the forces of nature, as did all the religions of the biblical world except Israelite Yahwism. Baal, the weather god, and Anat, his consort, were the central figures in Canaanite mythology and in the cultus to which it gave expression. The annual cycle of the seasons was believed to result from the waxing and waning of Baal's vitality. The rain ceased in summer and vegetation dried up because Baal died, and the rains came in autumn and winter and the earth became fertile again because Baal came back to life. It was

Anat who rescued him from death (the underworld, ruled by Mot, "Death"), and it was his mating with her which produced the fruits of earth and flock upon which human beings depended for survival. Thus, the salient moments in Canaanite religion were the subjugation of Baal by Death, his revivification by Anat, and his mating with the goddess.

Mosaic/prophetic Yahwism conflicted with Baalism in fundamental respects. It did not deify the powers of nature, but viewed them as religiously neutral aspects of God's creation, wholly dependent upon him for existence. Behind the creation was the one God, who was neither sexual nor mortal nor subject to any of the defects of creaturely existence. Unlike the nature-deities, he had not been born, and he did not marry or die. Nothing in creation could represent his being; therefore, no plastic images were to be made of him. Naturally, the central cultic dramas of Canaanite religion—lamentation over the death of the god, celebration of his resurrection, and enactment of the sacred marriage of god and goddess—were out of the question for Yahwism. Ritual prostitution, which was a concomitant of the myth and ritual of divine marriage, was anathema. In addition, there seems to have been a fundamental difference in the understanding of offerings made to the deity in the two religions. In the one they were believed to be required as the precondition of obtaining blessings from the gods, while in the other they were primarily expressions of gratitude for blessings already received.

The extant literature of the ancient Canaanites, which is very scant, says little about the ethical standards or moral sensibilities of the people. OT writers painted a dark picture of Canaanite morality, but they were probably biased in their perceptions and selective in their reports. Therefore, it would be unfair for us to judge Canaanite society from their account of it. We must also remember that the separation of Canaanite and Israelite was not nearly so sharp as the OT generally suggests. The ancestors of Israel descended from Canaanite and related peoples, and shared their religion and culture (cf. Josh 24:2, 14). All through the history of Israel to the exile there was intermingling and intermarriage among Israelite Yahwists and the non-Yahwistic peoples of Syria-Palestine. The military and political achievements of David and Solomon brought further diversity of population and religion to the new Israelite Kingdom. Thus the struggle between prophetic Yahwism and Canaanite Baalism was as much between the two religions of Israel as it was between a native and a foreign religion.

The fact that this religious conflict was an internal affair in Israel has several consequences for our interpretation of the OT. It makes the historical task of tracing the course of Israelite popular religion more difficult, but it brings the moral conflict between Yahwism and Baalism closer to us, for we can see mirrored in it the conflict in our own life between the traditional values of Judeo-Christian theism and those of a materialistic, sensual culture. This conflict occurs continually in the experience of everyone. It is a warfare waged within.

The ancient nature-religion was reasonable. As long as the gods were personified, as they were—are—in all popular religion, it was natural for the cycle of the seasons to be interpreted in terms of the great processes of human life: bisexual reproduction, life and death. So the myths—stories—which explained what happened annually to the earth, made sense. But these were not mere tales, told for entertainment or edification alone. They were the scenarios of worship, the substance and rationale of ritual, through which everyone could share in the great drama of life. It was unthinkable not to do so. The cosmic process was a partnership between human beings and the gods. Performance of the rituals was an indispensable contribution to the maintenance of order and the renewal of vitality in nature. There was an interdependence between gods and people in the vast struggle of life, and the cult—private and public sacrifices and ceremonies—was the point of meeting between divine and human forces. To neglect ritual was to place the whole enterprise in jeopardy. Religion was a matter of survival.

Today we are not as close to the earth as Israel and her neighbors were. Their agrarian-pastoral economy has long since given way to industrialism. Their mythic understanding of reality has been displaced by a scientific one. Much of the sacred has been secularized. The ritualism which controlled every phase of their life is gone. We no longer encounter nature as they did. Instead of personal, divine beings we perceive mechanical forces and impersonal processes, which have neither feeling nor understanding. These vast natural forces set limits to human life, shape and control it, enhance and destroy it, but without caring or purpose. Unhuman, impersonal, mechanical.

So we don't worship nature or try to manipulate it by ritual means. There are many individuals in our society who enjoy, and pursue, a kind of "communion with nature" in place of conventional religion, or in addition to it. However, this is usually esthetic appreciation rather than religion. It is non-cultic and non-corporate. It is more diversional than vocational, more poetic than pragmatic. This is not the modern correlative to Baalism.

The best analogies in our society to the fertility cult of ancient Canaan are materialism and sensualism. The evidence of these is everywhere in our culture, and it need not be catalogued here. We mean by these terms devotion to wealth and devotion to pleasure, the passionate pursuit of them. Wealth and pleasure are not evil in themselves, nor incompatible with faith in the God of Israel. Biblical religion is not unworldly or spiritualistic. The Bible affirms the goodness of creation, of matter and sense. Material things are good in themselves, including the human body. They are to be used and enjoyed. The resources of nature are gifts of God; they are not antithetical to godliness.

The conflict with faithfulness to God arises when the acquisition of wealth and the pursuit of pleasure begin to control us, to shape the course of our lives, to determine our priorities. Wealth and pleasure then assume a religious or quasi-religious significance and threaten to undermine our higher loyalties. They nourish self-centeredness and distract us from love of neighbor and concern for social justice. For those who reject traditional biblical faith there is no religious conflict in this, but for those who embrace that faith it is a profoundly religious matter.

This conflict occurs in each of us, although it takes many forms and has many outcomes. No one can judge another in this regard, although it is extremely tempting to do so. "Have nots" will tend to find these faults in the "haves," but materialism and sensualism are no respecters of persons. Crass examples are always available through the mass media, but the difficulty in using them for sermonic illustrations is that they are usually so far removed from the lives of most congregations that they fail to affect them personally. Headshaking at the deplorable state of society has little impact on people's decisions and style of life. No, the serious conflict is more subtle than this. It is a daily affair for everyone who is above a subsistence level economically. It is a question of private versus social values, of the allocation of resources, of stewardship and conservation. The outward form of the conflict is utterly different from what it was in ancient Israel—economically, politically, socially, technologically—but the moral and religious dimensions of it are similar. By using our imaginations we should be able to see ourselves and our culture mirrored in the allegorical figure of God's wife in Hos 2.

The interaction between Israelite Yahwism and Canaanite Baalism was complex. Much in Baalism was incompatible with Yahwism and had to be rejected. But other features of the nature-cult had a positive influence upon Israelite religion. Chief of these was the effort to comprehend the whole physical world in its relation to the human community. Israel could not omit the realm of nature from its theological concerns and still maintain faith in one God. All things had to be brought together into a single unity under one sovereign Lord. There was a danger in this, for Canaanite mythology and ritual would always have an enormous accessibility and appeal to unsophisticated people. Faith in one, transcendent, asexual, imageless God was harder to sustain, just as it is today! Nevertheless, it was a risk worth taking, for an adequate faith demanded it. Israel's interaction with Baalism meant both antagonism and accommodation. So it is in our time, in the interaction between religion and culture.

Modern readers may be repulsed by Hosea's marrying a prostitute or saddling his children with peculiar names. Indeed some interpreters of the Bible in recent generations have refused to take the accounts of Hos 1 and 3 literally. However, Hosea was not the only prophet to engage in such symbolic actions. Isaiah gave his children strange, prophetic names (Isa 7:3; 8:3) and paraded in public in his underwear (Isa 20), and Jeremiah and Ezekiel performed equally bizarre acts (Jer 13:1–7; Ezek 4–5). This was not mere eccentricity. It was total dedication to the word of God. The strangeness of these actions should not be explained away on the grounds that they were commonplace in the ancient world, an ordinary feature of the culture, for they seem to have been extraordinary then, too. On the other hand, there is no reason to take them as a general model for the dedicated servant of God. We should simply respect the quality of the prophets' commitment and the imagination and daring they showed in carrying it out.

At one point in particular we should recognize the discontinuity between the prophets' social situation and ours and beware of using them even indirectly as the norm of loyalty to God. This point is the way in which they brought their families into their service of the word. Modern parents do not have the right to impose their own religious vocations upon their children or spouses, as the Israelite prophets did theirs. There was a profound unity in the Hebrew family which does not exist today. The kind of personal freedom and independence we experience and nourish in our culture was unknown in Israel. There was nothing approaching the individualism which characterizes our life. Consequently, many things which were appropriate in their attitudes and behavior are not in ours. One of these is the subordination of wife and children to the vocation and interests of the husband/father. In Israel it would not have been experienced as subordination, but would have been accepted as natural and inevitable, and therefore desirable. In our society it is simply wrong.

No text in the Bible manifests faith in a loving God more than Hos 1 –3. God's relationship to his people is likened to the most intimate bond in human experience, that of wife and husband. The love denoted by this simile is both tender and responsible. It seeks love in return and yet requires righteousness as the condition of true life. It disciplines, forgives, and persists. It seeks, offers, and exhorts. It suffers and sustains. These are the qualities of God's love set forth by Hosea in these brief, compelling lines.

The Knowledge of God (4:1 –19)

Infidelity is rooted in the disposition of the heart. This is the opening message of Hos 4. Outward violations of personal relationships bespeak an inward deficiency of commitment or understanding. Hosea observed the prevalence of lying, killing, stealing, and adultery in Israel and saw beneath them a lack of devotion and knowledge of God (4:1 –2). He did not mention the covenant by name in these lines, nor did he continue here to use the marriage metaphor which dominates the first three chapters of the book; however, the insights expressed in chap 4 reflect the understanding of the covenant and of marriage which is presented in chaps 1 – 3.

The evils mentioned in 4:2 are similar to some of those prohibited by the Ten Commandments. "Killing, stealing, and committing adultery" are the identical crimes proscribed by the sixth, eighth, and seventh commandments, and there may be an allusion to the third or ninth commandment in the reference to "swearing and lying." It is uncertain exactly when the Ten Commandments received their final formulation in Israel's religious tradition. In the end the Decalogue became the summary of the obedience demanded by God of his people. It may have been recited regularly in covenantal ceremonies, and was probably taught to Israelite children as a kind of catechism. If such practices were common already in Hosea's time, as many scholars believe, it would have been natural for Hosea to refer to the Ten Commandments in this way. In doing so, he would have been pointing to a fundamental incongruity between precept and practice, between worship and daily life, in Israel's experience. Such hypocrisy in religion was not unique in the history of human culture! Moreover, the standard by which Hosea was judging Israel was not an ethic of perfection but merely one of basic human decency. He was referring to breaches of a minimal code of morality to which all reasonable people would subscribe. Therefore, his outrage was understandable.

People with a pre-scientific perspective—and there are many such people even today—tend to link the vicissitudes of nature with those of society. To Hosea, the blight he observed in the physical environment (4:3) was a consequence of the moral corruption of Israel. Fortunately, there is no simple correlation between these two realms. If there were, the cumulative weight of human evil across the millenia would have destroyed our planet long ago! Nevertheless, there is a point worth pondering in Hosea's poem. There is more validity in his assertion today than at any time in history. The fate of the earth is more nearly in human hands than ever before. We have the technological capacity to consume, pollute, and denude our world, even to make it lifeless. It has happened on a

small scale already. It could happen on a planetary scale, by
neglect and self-interest if not by conscious design. Nature's
blight is not caused by outbreaks of adultery and murder, as
Hosea's oracle implies, but there is some relationship between the way people treat each other and the way they treat
their environment. For this reason above all, the future of the
earth is indeed linked to the moral destiny of humankind.

The root of the problem, Hosea said, was the lack of
knowledge of God (4:1). Knowing God is unlike any other kind
of knowing, because there is nothing else like God; and yet
there are analogies to it in other forms of experience. It is most
like knowing another person, which involves cognitive aware-
ness, emotional involvement, and dynamic interchange between free, intelligent beings. It is not gained all at once, but
requires sustained engagement of thought, feeling, and will. It
is not superficial or casual, but central and ultimate. It shapes
attitudes, decisions, being. It is all-consuming, life-directing.
And, in Hosea's judgment, there was too little of it in Israel.

Who was to blame?

In the end, we are all responsible for our own knowledge
of God, and for the fidelity and devotion which express and
sustain it (4:1). No adult can be exonerated for the lack of such
knowledge, and Hosea exonerated no one. However, he did
single out some as especially culpable. These were the religious leaders of Israel, the priests and prophets (4:4–10). Not
only were they deficient themselves, but their failure contributed to that of others, for they carried a special responsibility
for religious education.

There were no Sunday schools in Hosea's time. Religious
education took place informally in the process of growing up
in an Israelite family, and more formally by participating in
the annual festivals and other acts of communal worship.
Israel's rituals made large use of animal sacrifice, but at their
best they also included the kind of verbal content which is
found in the book of Psalms, the Ten Commandments, and the
confessional recitals of the acts of God (Deut 26:5–10; Josh
24:2–15). Here the covenantal faith could be nourished and
renewed, and for those who were new to the Yahwistic community—children, resident aliens, newcomers, converts, foreign wives—an understanding of this faith could be learned
and appropriated. We do not know precisely what role the

priests and prophets had in teaching this faith, and its ethical corollaries, but we may conclude from Hosea's criticism of them (4:6) that it was substantial. If they neglected the task, the quality of worship was altered. It deteriorated into a quasi-magical system for placating God and buying his favors.

The system of sin-offerings was especially susceptible to abuse. Lev 4 –7 describes these sacrifices. The priests received a portion of them (Lev 7:7 –10, 28 –35), and this portion constituted a significant part of their income. Thus the priests had a vested interest in the people's sinning! Hosea says they fed upon it, longing for the people's offenses (4:8). There is an obvious parallel here to the sale of indulgences in the Medieval Christian Church. Modern abuses are perhaps more subtle, though there is no reason to believe they are any less common. The basic offense with which Hosea charged the priests was exploiting human need for their own profit. There is nothing wrong with being compensated for services performed, when a real need is being met. However, the implication of Hosea's charge is that the priests were neglecting the people's real need for instruction in covenantal faith and morality, while they were profiting from rituals which had little value. They soothed the troubled consciences of individuals, but contributed nothing to human relations or the social order.

One of the main attractions of Baalism, and of baalized Yahwism, was sacred prostitution. It persisted in Israel until the fall of the two kingdoms. Hosea blamed the men for it and exonerated the women (4:13 –14). This imbalance of blame may have been a bit extreme, but it was basically fair in a society dominated by males. Prostitution among women in our society is a different matter. Women share much more than ancient Israelite women did in controlling social policy, and they have more freedom to determine the course of their own lives. Therefore, whatever blame is to be assigned for prostitution in our society, or for other forms of sexual exploitation, belongs to women as well as men. Curiously, today we tend to blame only the prostitutes or "sexploiters" themselves, although this is hardly just. Quite apart from the question of indirect responsibility for a complex social phenomenon, direct responsibility belongs to both the purveyors and the consumers. Some cities in the United States have laws punishing both

prostitutes and their clients. Surely, if the seller is to be punished, it seems only fair to punish the buyer as well (though
we may wonder how effective such laws really are). In any
case, it is interesting to find an echo of Hosea's words in a social debate of our own time.

Hosea mentioned adultery as well as prostitution (4:14).
This is a more important matter because it affects many more
people. Hosea said nothing new about the act itself (he was
against it!). His point was merely to insist that in Israel men
were more culpable for it than women. We would not try to
make this point today, although we still deplore adultery. In
our society women share equal guilt for it with men.

Hosea did not call for the equality of women with men or
the "liberation" of women. Indeed, he advocated discrimina-
tory judgment in the case of adultery by suggesting that men
deserved to be treated more harshly than women. The obvious
principle behind his opinion was that of fairness. The larger
issue of the fairness of the status of women in Israelite society
was never raised. It was probably never imagined by Hosea or
his contemporaries.

The relation of inward disposition to outward behavior is
a theme running through Hos 4. The chapter begins with a
general indictment of the Israelite people for their lack of
faithfulness, devotion, and religious knowledge (4:1). Two of
the recent English versions translate this line especially well.
The NEB reads, "There is no good faith or mutual trust, or
knowledge of God in the land," and the NJV, "There is no hon-
esty and no goodness and no obedience to God in the land."
Another spirit possesses the people's hearts, namely the "spirit of harlotry" (4:12). Their destructive, idolatrous deeds issue
from this "spirit," this inner quality. Their affections and
their wills are in bondage to alien "gods"; therefore, their outward behavior inevitably reflects this bondage. A change in
behavior requires a change of heart. But how can this come
about? Obviously, not by taking thought. Education by precept is not enough. One has to want to learn! More radical
means are required. In Hosea's opinion this meant national
exile—a stern means of discipline and instruction!

The reform of a society usually requires a crisis or disaster to bring it about. This is sometimes true of individuals as
well. However, individuals have much more freedom of the

will than groups or nations do. Hosea's unit of consideration was a large community; therefore, it is on the communal level that his insights can best be applied. Nevertheless, they have a bearing also on individual lives.

Hos 4 shows in a series of vivid, poetic scenes how evil hearts produce evil deeds. There is no denying that this analysis is true to experience. But it is only half of the truth about human behavior, for evil deeds also produce evil hearts. There is a reciprocal relationship between affections and attitudes, on the one hand, and acts, on the other. It prevails in good as well as evil behavior. Thus, there is a point to remedial discipline, even for the hardened will. Education can contribute to the formation of the heart and will, just as legislation can contribute to the change of communal attitudes, even though it cannot bring this about by itself. Religious education cannot assure the inception of faith, but it can contribute to it. The knowledge of God cannot simply be taught, but an environment can be created in which it is stimulated and supported.

Hos 4:1-19 shows what can happen to a society that does not know God. This is the major theme of the chapter. It is as preachable today as it was in Hosea's day, although the illustrations may have to be changed. Lack of faith (religious experience, knowledge of God) brings disregard of fundamental moral principles (4:1-2). Social relations are corrupted and religion becomes hypocrisy. This is all negative, but turn it around and observe that the opposite results flow from genuine knowledge of God.

The Absent God (5:1-15)

None of Israel's leaders were exempt from Hosea's indictment. In chap 4 he dealt with the religious leaders; here in chap 5 he broadens the charge to include the political leaders as well.

The chapter falls into two main parts. Part one (5:1-7) opens with a summons to trial before God (5:1-2). It names the defendants and summarizes the crime, and the intended punishment. Then the indictment (5:3-5) and the sentence (5:6-7) are spelled out in greater detail. Part two (5:8-15) describes an international conflict between Israel and Judah and interprets it as God's punishment of the two unrighteous nations. Both sections of the chapter conclude with an assertion that God will abandon them (5:6 and 14). When they seek him he will be gone!

The problem with Israel's leaders was that they had reversed the order of means and ends. They were supposed to be agents of justice (the JB translates the crucial line in v 1, "You who are responsible for justice"), servants of the covenant-people, and thus servants of God. But they had turned their positions into means for satisfying their own interests. In the prophets' view, they had become exploiters of the people—predators, trapping the people as game (5:1)!

In any political office (national or ecclesiastical) there is the temptation to use its authority and power for the benefit of the one who holds it. It is easy to lose sight of the constituency or society which the office is supposed to serve. Failure to resist this temptation is common enough in elective offices, or ones of limited term. In offices like the priesthood and kingship in ancient Israel, both of which were hereditary and life-long, the temptation to such abuse must have been overwhelming. It is amazing that there were ever any disinterested, dedicated priests or kings!

There was a close tie between these two offices in Israel. The kingship was regarded as sacred, and many occasions in a king's life were celebrated ritually. This was true of positive occasions—birth (Isa 9:2–7), coronation (Ps 2), marriage (Ps 45), military triumph (Ps 18)—but also of negative ones. When a king, or the kingship itself, was threatened, the aid and succor of Almighty God were sought (Pss 20, 21, 89). The king was believed to be the chosen vice-regent of God, ruling for him in the midst of his people, and even among the nations (Pss 2; 72:8–11; 89:22–27). He might lose divine support temporarily if he broke the commandments of God, but he would never lose it entirely (Ps 89:30–37). Repentance and sacrifice provided the necessary and sufficient means to restore a broken relationship with God.

Hos 5:1–7 depicts the leaders of Israel in just such a ritual effort to assuage their guilt and restore their relationship with God. However, Hosea declares the effort to be futile. "Ephraim shall stumble in his guilt" (5:5), and when he seeks God at the sanctuary, ready to placate him with whole herds of sacrificial beasts, he will not find him (5:6). God will be gone!

This is highly anthropomorphic imagery. It scandalizes the religious imagination. If God is present always and everywhere, then it is not appropriate to speak about God's absence. To do so makes God appear too much like a human being, coming and going. Perhaps so. However, Hosea used bold poetic images of God, not only as human, but as "subhuman." We encounter some of the boldest of these in this chapter, where God is likened to a ravaging lion (5:14) and to disease and decay (5:12, see NJV and NEB). So Hosea, like most of the biblical writers, filled his religious discourse with graphic metaphors, in order to heighten the effect of his oracles. This certainly made them more memorable!

His point, of course, was not that God was really absent—indeed, the God who ravages like a lion or a wasting disease is only too present!—but that he was not available to be used in the way the Israelite worshippers wished. God as they imagined him was not there. He was not at their disposal.

The political leaders in our nation are not sacral figures as the kings of ancient Israel were, and our government is constitutionally forbidden to subsidize religion. Therefore, the worst excesses of the Israelite leaders in using religion for political ends are avoided in our society. Nevertheless, there are subtler ways in which this is done. But the message of the prophets is clear. Whether the effort is gross or subtle, the attempt to claim the power of God for partisan interests will ultimately fail. The leaders of a people must finally serve the people or God will "abandon" them. Abandonment does not take the form of the departure of an anthropomorphic spiritual power. It works through the process of political and social interaction. It may take a long time. However, Hosea and his prophetic peers were convinced that where government and religion do not support the cause of popular justice, the system of rule will perish, together with its ritual sanctions. This conviction was confirmed in the history of Israel, and it is worth pondering in the churches of today.

Hos 5:8–15 is a tale of violent brotherly strife. Israel and Judah had warred against each other off and on for two centuries, for the usual reasons: land, trade, food, political superiority. Hosea's oracle reflects the last phase of this internecine conflict about a decade before the fall of the northern Israelite kingdom. We need not trace the details of this war. There are three main points that we should observe. First, Israel and Judah were sister peoples who traced their lineage to the same Sinaitic covenant. However, much of their history under the monarchy had been lived in violation of this bond and the common destiny it implied. Second, both kingdoms were willing to use outside forces against each other (5:14). Third, these policies contributed to the fall of Israel and the decline of Judah. In Hosea's perspective the result was well deserved.

Few economic or social problems are solved by the use of violence. Revolutions and civil wars leave evils in their wake that may be worse than the ones which preceded them. Governments and armies usually believe God is on their side in the struggle against rival claimants to power, territory, and wealth. For Hosea, the blessing of God could not be claimed by any of the participants in the wars of his time. As the source of creative power God was absent from the international scene. He was present only as the judge of unrighteousness—a lion who tore apart his prey and then retired to his den.

There may be occasions when violence is necessary to establish justice, but most of the time it undermines it. Moral and social wellbeing are achieved by other means.

A suggested topic for preaching on Hos 5 is, "When Being Religious Is an Offense to God." Popular religion and biblical faith are not the same thing. The power of God is not available for exploitation. If our cause is antithetical to God's cause, we may find emptiness at the end of our quest (5:6), or, worse, the actual frustration of our purposes (5:14–15). The power of God is always available. This is the prophetic faith. However, the conditions that must be met in order to receive it are determined by God and not ourselves.

Revival on the Third Day (6:1–6)

God can be known as surely in worship as in any realm of experience. For the people of the covenant he is not known truly without the sustained experience of corporate worship. And yet worship can become shallow and illusory. A fickle, "fox-hole" religion, unaccompanied by disciplined obedience to the moral tenets of the covenant, is ultimately vain. It is self-serving; therefore, it is self-defeating.

Hos 6:1–3 is a splendid affirmation of the renewing power of God, which is available to his people in their great rituals. We can imagine the pilgrims to one of the annual festivals of Israel (Exod 23:14– 17), singing a psalm in words like these, confident that at the end of their pilgrimage—"on the third day"—they would experience anew the lifegiving joy of religious celebration. Although they had been punished by God for their sins, they could count on his forgiveness and healing (v. 1).

Their doctrine was true, but their practice falsified it. In the circumstances, God could only continue to judge them (v. 5). This judgment was partly the function of prophetic preaching, as this preaching correlated with the tragic events of Israel's unfolding history. The prophetic word was a perennial testimony to the conditions of genuine revival, and to the consequences of failure to fulfill these conditions.

The forgiveness of God is always available. This is a fundamental premise of the sacrificial system of the OT, just as it is a central element of the NT gospel. However, healing and renewal (v. 1), if they are to have any significant or lasting effect upon the quality of human relationships, involve sustained commitment. The people must *work* for social wholeness, finding the fulfillment of their personal needs in the good of the community—discovering their own health in active concern for the wellbeing of others.

Modern worship is as subject to abuse and misunderstanding as worship in ancient Israel. The great "pilgrimage festivals" of the church year—Christmas and Easter—as well as the sacramental feast of the Lord's Supper and other acts of worship, can be perceived and experienced individualistically and selfishly, despite the long tradition of the Church's teaching about their true meaning. We all have continual need of the prophetic word—"hewing" and "slaying" (v. 5) our pride and selfishness, again and again and again. We may assume that the word of the gospel guarantees our rituals to be authentic Christian worship. However, in the urgency of our personal religious need, we may lose sight of the prophetic dimension of that word. This dimension is two-fold. It is both criticism and exhortation, and it is always social, not merely in the narrow sense that each individual life is lived in relation to other persons, but in the wider sense that the life of each person is bound up with the lives of all the people of God. There are no limits to the extent of this bond, either in space or in time. Every worshiping congregation is a part of the enduring, world-wide covenant-community. Therefore, it cannot be concerned solely with its own needs, but must concern itself with the sufferings and aspirations of the whole people of God. Nor is this people only those in religious communities, who share a common faith or institutional structure. As God is one, and the God of all creation, so humankind is ultimately one community. Constancy of love, which is the test of true religion (v. 6), means love of God's people, as well as love of God. The Baalism to which our fickle hearts turn again and again is not only disregard of the true God. It is also disregard of other people. Social responsibility is an essential component of authentic faith.

Paul the apostle's affirmation that Jesus was raised "on the third day, in accordance with the scriptures" (1 Cor 15:4) appears to be an allusion to Hos 6:2. If so, there is a certain appropriateness to the statement. The similarity of times is not so important, although this is probably what led Paul, and others in the early church, to make the connection. More significant, however, is the similarity of substance in the two events. In both, the faithful discern the forgiveness and life-giving power of God. The Christian witness centers on the person of Jesus, but it presupposes the same understanding of God as the OT confession of faith. This confession is characterized memorably in the words which Hosea quotes. As we have already said, these words in themselves are a valid affirmation of faith. Hosea's quarrel with his coreligionists is not over this affirmation. Rather, it concerns their moral infidelity. In the face of this, the judgment of God, which they have already experienced, can only be suffered again. But God's willingness to forgive and his capacity to give new life are as constant as their obedience is inconstant. Therefore, their confession can be taken up by Christian readers today, united with the apostolic faith in Christ's triumph over sin and death, and proclaimed anew in our own generation.

It is a bold faith expressed in Hos 6:1–3. The people turn for healing to the very one who wounded them! But God the chastiser is God the healer. There is only one God. The whole of our experience is grounded in his love, his righteousness, and his power. There is no possibility of appeal to a second deity against the righteous claims of the one, nor is there any need for such an appeal. The justice of God is an aspect of his concern for the wellbeing of all his creatures. It is based in his love. The forgiveness of God is necessary because we violate—or neglect—the claims of his righteousness—finite, selfish, ignorant creatures that we are. Justice and forgiveness sometimes seem incompatible with each other, but both are manifestations of the love of God. Love is not static and mechanical, but dynamic and personal. It is responsive, creative, living. God in his love requires our commitment to love others, which means, among other things, obedience to the moral principles of the covenant and concern for social justice. Without these, there can be no corporate fulfillment for the people of God. But God in his love is always ready to forgive his sinful people, to enable us to begin again, to live again, to find fulfillment in a community of righteousness and mutual love.

We don't sacrifice animals or burn offerings today, so we must translate Hos 6:6 into other terms. What we do, in most efforts at religious revival, is stimulate feelings. Feeling good about ourselves and God—many Christians speak about feeling close to Jesus—is not a bad thing. But the measure of a true relationship with God, and of any authentic religious revival, is "steadfast love" (6:6), as it is manifest in the quality of one's life.

Faith and/or Politics (6:7 –7:16)

During the last twenty years of its existence, the Kingdom of Israel fell into social chaos. The biblical account of the story is a mere outline (2 Kgs 15:8 –31 and 17:1 –6), but it is highly indicative. King Zechariah was assassinated by Shallum ben Jabesh after six months on the throne. One month later Shallum was murdered by Menahem ben Gadi. Menahem managed to hold the throne for about ten years by means of Assyrian support. He was remembered as the one who butchered the men, women, and children of a city in his own kingdom, because they refused to acknowledge his sovereignty! (2 Kgs 15:16). His son Pekahiah succeeded him for two years and was then assassinated by Pekah ben Remaliah. Pekah is best known for his misguided attack upon the sister Kingdom of Judah (2 Kgs 16:5; Isa 7:1 –9). He was assassinated in his turn by Hoshea ben Elah. Hoshea renewed Israel's vassalage to Assyria, but caused the kingdom's final destruction by conspiring with Egypt. Such is the sorry tale of the last days of Israel. This is the immediate background of Hos 6– 7!

The prophets may have exaggerated the evils of their society. At least, they tell us nothing about good and true acts performed by their compatriots, and it is incredible that none were performed! Nevertheless, the prophets were all in agreement about what was wrong with life in Israel and Judah. We may assume that their picture was incomplete, but we may accept it as authentic. Hos 6– 7, then, and other passages, help to fill in the outline of Israel's history given in 2 Kgs.

The passage before us catalogues evils which Hosea regarded as epidemic in the Kingdom of Israel. Some of the details are obscure (the text is difficult to make sense of at some points), but the general meaning of the indictment is plain enough. Treachery and conspiracy were rampant among the religious and political leaders. Trust was gone. Personal safety was constantly threatened. Violence was common. Rulers rose and fell. The picture is one of desperation, even panic.

The trouble was not confined to domestic affairs, but reached also to foreign relations. Alliances were made and broken, first with one nation and then with another (7:8– 11). Nothing worked to stabilize the kingdom. Indeed, international politics served only to deepen the chaos within.

What remedy is there for a society in such turmoil? Legal reform? Education? Governmental control? Religion? Each of these, and other measures, can contribute to constructive social change in many circumstances. However, when the leadership of a nation is deeply implicated in the evil that threatens it, there is not much hope for reform. It is then ripe for revolution—or conquest. Hosea was convinced that his nation was doomed to conquest. As other oracles in the book show (1:10– 2:1; 2:14– 23; 3:5; 11:10– 11; 14:1– 7), he did not believe the fall of Israel would mean extinction for the people of God. However, he saw no hope for the current institutions and leadership of the kingdom. Only out of the death of the kingdom could new life come for the covenant-community.

Several lines in this section of the book seem to suggest a contrast between faith in God and political activity, which may induce some modern readers to separate these two

realms of life in their own minds. Hos 7:7, 13 – 16, are the lines
in question. Read in one way, they might be taken to set faith
in God over against political involvement as incompatible
modes of behavior. Is this a correct interpretation, and, if so,
does it have a bearing upon the relation of faith to political activity in our own lives?

Hos 7:7 should be dealt with separately from 7:13– 16.
The point of v. 7 is that the king-makers in Israel are faithless
men who destroy their rulers as fast as they create them. They
are villains with totally selfish motives. No general theory of
the proper bearing of faith in God upon political action is suggested in this part of Hosea's oracle.

Hos 7:13– 16 is a somewhat different matter. Here it is
suggested that authentic Yahwism and the kind of international politics played by the leaders of Israel are incompatible. However, this does not mean that reliance upon God is a
simple alternative to reliance upon foreign nations, that is,
that faith necessarily excludes all international alliances for a
Yahwistic community or nation.

Hosea was saying that Israel's relations with Egypt and
Assyria in his own time constituted a rebellion against
Yahweh. This kingdom was both a national state and a religious community. Government and cultus were interdepen-
dent, and both were controlled by an absolute, hereditary
monarch, whose authority derived from a doctrine of divine
rule and whose power resided in a standing army of professional soldiers. In these circumstances, justice and religion
were easily corrupted. Religion was readily made the servant
of the king. Maintenance of the power of the court required a
considerable share of the nation's wealth and served to widen
the gap between the privileged class and the majority of the
people. Cult and government were intertwined in every nation, so international relations, especially with the great nations whose favor was most curried, often led to the
introduction of foreign ideas and practices into the religious
life of Israel. Yahweh came to be regarded merely as the local
god of Israel rather than the supreme power in the world. This
reduction in the sense of Yahweh's importance meant also a
diminished regard for the ethical principles of the Yahwistic
covenant. Traditional Israelite morality and concern for social justice were eroded. Thus at every level, outward and in-

ward, Israel's life was threatened by a tyrannical and idolatrous leadership.

The separation of church and state in our society is a safeguard against the evils which resulted from the commingling of the two realms in ancient Israel. However, modern religious communities are as subject to syncretism and apostasy as Hosea's contemporaries were, and modern states are still subject to idolatry and tyranny. International relations today do not involve the same compromise of religious loyalties as in the ancient world of absolute monarchs and state religions, although religious zeal can infect the struggle for power among nations and groups, as the recent history of Northern Ireland and the Middle East shows. Faith can become fanaticism when linked with a political cause. This is the danger on one side. The danger on the other side is that faith and politics be so divorced that the conduct of public life is cut off from the deepest roots of morality. Avoiding these extremes is a continual obligation of those who would stand in the prophetic tradition.

A King for the People (8:1 – 14)

Everyone wants leaders who understand their struggle for life and offer them hope for its enhancement. The surest way for a leader to understand his people's sufferings and aspirations is to share them. A leader who has risen from the people or participated with them directly in the events which led to a new order in their lives has a bond with them which can survive all sorts of mistakes and weaknesses on the leader's part. The stories of Moses and David illustrate the point. There are many modern examples that could be given also, of leaders as different as George Washington and Mao Tse Tung. But those who follow later in the line of leadership may not have this natural bond of shared origin or experience. They may merely inherit the throne, figuratively or literally.

In Hosea's Israel, both kingship and priesthood were hereditary. Close ties with the people, wisdom and generosity were not necessary qualifications for office. Whether a king or priest served the people's needs and represented them truly in the affairs of state was a matter of individual disposition and choice on the part of the leader. The impression we are given by the OT accounts is that many of the kings and priests of Israel lacked the ability or sympathy to serve the people properly. The order of ends and means was reversed. Kings who in Yahwism were supposed to be servants became mere dynasts, exploiting the people for their own purposes. Therefore, the prophet could declare rightly, on God's behalf, "They made kings, but not through me!" (Hos 8:4).

The accountability of leaders is a crucial matter in any society or institution. In ancient Israel the kings were held accountable to God, but everyone can rationalize their behavior as being in accord with God's will, while actually serving their own interests primarily. There must be external checks imposed by the community and some accepted means of terminating a ruler's tenure in office. A leader who cannot be fired cannot be held accountable. Israel had no orderly means of choosing and replacing kings. She had to suffer under an unlimited, hereditary monarch.

Democratic institutions have replaced the monarchy in our culture, so many of the evils associated with kingship have been eliminated from our life. The issue that this chapter of Hosea calls us to consider, then, is whether the leaders of the communities to which we belong are sufficiently accountable to the people they are supposed to serve. Do all the people have a voice in choosing their leaders or some alternative means of assuring that their needs are met and their opinions respected? This question is important to ask of churches as well as governments. In modified form it even applies to families, businesses, and schools. What does it mean to create and tolerate leaders, "but not through [God]!"? Conversely, what ethical principles ought to control the structures of authority which order our many communities? The specific answers we give to these questions will vary from place to place and time to time, but the asking is a responsibility of every segment of the people of God.

The images of God used in the Israelite cult reflected the sacral kingship. God was conceived as King and represented as such. According to Hosea (8:4–5) this representation was influenced by the iconography of Canaanite Baalism. Yahweh was thought of as the warrior king, Baal, riding on a bull. Yahweh himself may not have been depicted in human form, as Baal was in the alien cult; nevertheless, the borrowed imagery lent itself to idolatry. This, too, the prophet Hosea decried.

Christian imagery today does not include the bull calf of Samaria. However, there are aspects of our image of God which can be idolatrous. Chief among these is the notion that God is male. It is an idea that all of us deny when we ask ourselves whether we actually believe that God is male, but our religious consciousness is affected by it just the same. Having addressed God as Father and Lord all our lives, we find it difficult to give an equal place to feminine images in our thinking about the divine.

Our ideas of God affect our human relationships. A society that thinks of God as masculine will depreciate the feminine wherever it appears. The inequality of the sexes in our culture, and the injustices perpetrated against women, are inspired and sustained by a belief in God as father. It is true that we need to speak of God in the metaphors of human relationship in order to keep God personal; yet all personal metaphors are limiting if they are absolutized. This is as true of the metaphor of father as it is of that of king, judge, or warrior.

Hosea declaimed, "A workman made it! It is not God!" (8:5). It is easy to shield ourselves against this barb by supposing it to be aimed only at the bronze calf in the old Israelite temple. In reality, though, it can be directed against all our images of God. Any one of them becomes an idol if it is made absolute.

Three things are denounced in this chapter of Hosea: absolute monarchy, idolatrous cult imagery, and sacrifices for sin. In Hosea's judgment, the system of sacrifices which was supposed to provide atonement for sin was actually contributing to the nation's guilt (8:11). There are several possible reasons for such a judgment. There may have been a lot of "cheap grace" dispensed by the temple, that is, assurance of forgiveness without real repentance. Or, priests and worshippers may have been indifferent to social justice. Or, the ritual of the temple may have been corrupted by pagan practices such as sacred prostitution.

What are the equivalents of these abuses in our own worship? The first, hypocrisy, is as much a trait of our religion as it was of ancient Israel's. Indifference to social justice is also thoroughly modern. We manage to avoid the cruder forms of eroticism, but, in its subtler forms, it is not absent from contemporary religion.

Hosea's stricture leaves us wondering how a religious community ought to deal ritually with sin and guilt. Manipulation of animal blood is not the answer, but what do we do instead? Some congregations resist giving a significant place in their liturgies to acts of confession and forgiveness. These can become perfunctory, or morbid. However, there are ample resources in the heritage of Christian worship to provide meaningfully for this indispensable corporate need. As individuals we sometimes need private counsel to deal with our guilt; but this is done more adequately when we are members of a community which acknowledges this aspect of human experience and responds to it with the seriousness and compassion which characterize the biblical witness.

Modern ministers may be put off by Hos 8, since the kings and king-like idols it talks about do not exist in our society. How does one preach from a text like that?

The issue underlying this chapter is a fundamental one which applies to all socio-political systems and the religious attitudes that accompany them. We tend to deify the forms of leadership to which we are accustomed and, at the same time, to conceive of God in similar terms. Thus, desirable social change is inhibited and our understanding of God is limited. Prophetic preaching cannot remedy these ills by itself, but preaching which is not prophetic contributes to them. We need Hosea as guide and spur even though we must adapt his message to our own situation.

Perversity of Root and Branch (9:1–17)

Virtue and vice may not be transmitted from one generation to another, but their consequences often are. A century after Hosea, Jeremiah's hearers complained that "the fathers have eaten sour grapes and the children's teeth are set on edge" (Jer 31:29). The complaint was valid, and it would have applied as well to Israel in 722 B.C. as to Judah in 587. One generation *does* suffer for the sins and follies of its forebears, though it also benefits from their wisdom and success. The suffering of the innocent for the sins of their parents is never so evident, and so complete, as in war or political conquest. Hosea's prophetic vision was of Israel's conquest and exile;

therefore, we must understand his prediction of the slaughter of Israelite children (9:11 – 13) as historical realism and not as a personal wish.

As we view our own experience as parents, or as the children of our parents, we know some of the destructive effects of generational continuity, although few of us see our children having to pay as huge a price for their parent's sins as the Israelite children of 722 B.C. had to pay. Happily the possibilities of grace are almost always sufficient to compensate for our mistakes, and provide our children with chance after chance. Also, the self-determining being of each individual person makes it possible for children to resist parental control and rise above social conditioning. In most families it is not inevitable that the sins of the parents be visited upon the children to the third and fourth generation.

What is true of individuals and families is not necessarily true of communities and nations. On this level the destiny of one generation—or three or four—may indeed be determined by the decisions and behavior of another. Furthermore, the basic mores, values, and patterns of social relationship which constitute a human culture, persist for centuries and shape the consciousness and behavior of all who live within it. A civilization does not change—cannot be changed—suddenly. This persistence of fundamental cultural values was acknowledged—and, in this case, deplored—by Hosea, in the oracle before us. He put it in different words, of course. For him, the earliest Israelites abandoned Yahweh, the savior who had "found (them) in the wilderness," and devoted themselves to Baal (9:10). The harlot's disposition which controlled the first generation of the new nation continued to control those which followed, right up to Hosea's time. Therefore, it was certain in his mind that the nation would eventually come to ruin, and the people be exiled from their ancestral land (9:3, 17).

Hosea called it "Yahweh's land" and contrasted it with the lands of Egypt and Assyria (9:3). Calling a land Yahweh's could mean several things. It might mean that Yahweh was believed to have residence, power, or effectiveness primarily, or exclusively, in this part of the earth; or it might mean that this land, like everything in Yahweh's creation, belonged to him and was made available for human use but not for human possession. By contrasting "Yahweh's land" with Assyria and

Egypt, Hosea's statement seems to imply the former meaning. This view of Yahweh's sphere of activity is reflected elsewhere in the Bible, for example in the plaintive cry of one of the psalmists, "How can we sing Yahweh's song in a foreign land?" (Ps 137:4). The answer to the question was given by Jeremiah when he told the Judean exiles in 598 that they could find Yahweh if they sought him earnestly, even in so alien a land as Babylonia (Jer 29:11 – 13). We would like to believe that Hosea held a similar conviction, but there is nothing sufficiently explicit in his writings to tell us whether or not he did.

Hosea's point was not the theological one of whether God was more accessible in one place than in another. Rather, he was asserting that Israel's exile from the land where the worship of Yahweh had been established would mean the cessation of that worship, together with all the benefits that flowed from it. For many Israelites this would seem like the end of their relationship with Yahweh.

This is the point which challenges the sensibilities of modern church people. Does our relationship with God require the forms of religious practice we are accustomed to, forms which are sanctified by a particular group or denomination? If our answer is really yes (the answer of our behavior, not that of our rationalizations), we may need the sort of rude awakening which Israel experienced in exile.

The other issue suggested by the reference to "Yahweh's land" is that of stewardship. In prophetic Yahwism, land is gift, as are all aspects of God's creation. It is held in trust as the material basis of a just and faithful society. It is not an outright possession, to be exploited for the selfish purposes of the ruling classes or the wealthy. It could be argued that Israel's loss of the land was the ultimate consequence of its misappropriation by these groups. At least this was the prophets' view.

The parallel to our modern situation is obvious, though now the issue is global. It is also much more complex. Stewardship is more than a private matter for individuals or groups. It is a matter of international responsibility, involving everyone who owns or uses natural resources. Stewardship of talents and opportunities is also an important ethical issue, and it is related to the one involved in Hos 9. However, it is the land that is at issue here.

Ancient prophets did not have the wisdom to solve the economic and political problems of their nation. Neither do modern preachers. We will look in vain in the oracles of Hosea and his fellow prophets for constructive proposals of policy in these areas. It was not their vocation to be statesmen. By the same token, we cannot expect ministers today to have solutions for complex socio-economic problems related to land and natural resources: problems of food, fuel, land-use, timber, water-rights, pollution, to name only the most obvious issues. Since these issues are far too complex to be solved even hypothetically by single individuals, everyone trying to speak prophetically about them should beware of simplistic allegations of blame or simplistic solutions. At the same time, it is very important for these issues to be discussed in the light of biblical faith and ethics. In the perspective of that faith it would be irresponsible for the people of God to be uninvolved in such discussion or the social action that flows from it.

Hos 9 falls into three main parts. Prophetic judgment permeates all three, but each has its distinctive features as well. Vv. 1 – 7a concern Israel's harvest-festival and Hosea's prediction that the people will soon be deprived of such celebrations. Vv. 7b – 9 describe the people's rejection of prophetic criticism and their hatred of the "watchman" in their midst. Vv. 10 – 17 conclude the oracle in the form of a dialogue of doom between Yahweh (vv. 10 – 13, 15 – 16) and the prophet (vv. 14 and 17).

Prophets are usually without honor in their own country. Most of the OT prophets were maligned or persecuted, and their message was always unpopular. We can understand this, for we are as resistant to criticism or moral admonition as the ancient Israelites were. Prophets anger us and arouse our hatred, too (v. 7). On the other side, prophets are fully human. They are just as subject to anger and hostility as anyone else. We see this in Hosea in his fierce petition to God to give his adversaries "a miscarrying womb and dry breasts" (9:14). It is not easy to speak the truth in love! No easier than to hear it. It is tempting for prophets to fall silent in order to avoid such conflict and such distressing feelings; but to be silent about evil and injustice is to abandon one's commitment to the covenant of God.

We have already noted that Hosea's use of the metaphors of root and branch and of human reproduction in this chapter have to do with the persistence of the consequences of sin from generation to generation. There is another level of meaning in this poetic imagery which should be noted as well. It is the relation of inward and outward behavior. Branches are to roots, and children are to parents, as deeds are to hearts. As the mind, motives, attitudes, affections, loyalties, and habits go, so go behavior and social relationships. We are known by our fruits, but those fruits issue from our inner selves. If the self is faithful its acts will be just. This is the message of Hos 4:1–3, and it is repeated in different terms in Hos 9.

Ruined Fortresses, Deserted Temples (10:1–15)

Over abandoned altars, thistles grow (10:8). This image of deserted temples, which was conjured up by Hosea in the eighth century B.C., can be matched in our own time by the real images of deserted abbeys in England and boarded-up churches in the inner cities of America. This is in the realm of religion. Here the prophet's message is: There is no abiding sanctuary. In the realm of military security, his message is that there is no impregnable fortress, no lasting refuge (10:14). The analogous images for our own time do not correspond as directly in the military realm as they do in the religious, but the memory of the United States' intervention in the Vietnamese War is one that can be cited. It evokes in us the same sense of futility today as Hosea's picture of ruined fortresses did in his time.

There are many possible ways of defining the issues which are suggested by these powerful, negative images in the poetry of Hosea. One way of doing so is to weigh the importance of expenditures for arms against those for such things as health, education, and economic development. In the realm of religion, the issue is frequently posed as a contrast between money for buildings and money for programs and people. If there is no abiding sanctuary, why build expensive churches, and if there is no enduring fortress, why persist in the arms race?

Congregations cannot serve people without buildings in which to meet, and nations cannot meet human needs without the means of preventing anarchy and invasion. Therefore,

it is artificial to set programs versus buildings, or welfare versus arms, as if these were mutually exclusive. In each case it is
a matter of achieving a proper balance among complex, inter-
dependent realities. Simple moral judgments are seldom useful in these realms. Nevertheless, the oracles of the prophets
can serve as helpful reminders to congregations and governments to reexamine their priorities in the light of the ultimate
human values which they are committed to serve.

Hosea, like most of the prophets, was an unremitting critic of the religious and political establishment in Israel. Although there were great achievements in both religion and
statecraft during the half-millennium of Israel's history up to
Hosea's time, Hosea characterizes the entire era as one of idolatry, apostasy, dissoluteness, tyranny, and oppression. If our
knowledge of Israel were derived only from the books of the
prophets, we might wonder whether there were any decent
people in the nation! It requires an act of creative imagination
to realize that this is a very one-sided picture. We must understand this imbalance in the prophetic assessment of Israel's
life in terms of the purpose of prophetic oracles. They were not
meant to provide a complete, accurate and well-rounded
description of the nation and its social institutions. Their purpose was to provoke the people, and especially their leaders,
to self-examination and repentance, and to stimulate moral
reformation and recommitment to the principles of the
Yahwistic covenant.

Chap 10 may be divided into two principal parts. Part one
(10:1 – 8) contains four strophes. The first (vv. 1 – 2) concerns
ritual; the second (vv. 3 – 4), kingship; the third (vv. 5 – 6),
Israel's cult image; and the fourth (vv. 7 – 8) unites these
themes in a kind of coda. Part two (10:9 – 15) is largely a
prophecy of the Israelite Kingdom's military defeat. In the
center of this part there is a powerful saying on justice and injustice, which is one of the most memorable sayings in the
prophetic literature (vv. 12 – 13).

Hosea's assessment of the monarchy was entirely negative. His way of saying that the institution was fundamentally
inimical to Israel's life under the covenant was to assert that it
was already evil in its very beginnings in Gibeah (9:9; 10:9).
His allusions to the days at Gibeah in these two passages seem
to point to the establishment of the kingship of Saul. Thus

from the beginning it was misguided and wrong. Thus the judgment which was made in 8:4 ("They made kings, but not through me. They set up princes, but without my knowledge") was meant to apply not only to the kings of the eighth century, but to the whole history of the monarchy in Israel.

The negative evaluation presented in the Book of Hosea is not the only view of monarchy contained in the OT. We also find positive and mixed interpretations there. The positive view is presented most clearly and forcefully in the Royal Psalms (Pss 2, 18, 20, 21, 45, 72, 89, 110, and 144). Here kingship is regarded as an institution ordained by God for the governance of his people. Although individual men may prove to be better or worse in their fulfillment of the royal responsibilities, and be judged by God accordingly, the institution itself is everlasting. This conviction was deeply held by many ancient Israelites, especially in the southern Kingdom of Judah, and it provided the foundation for the later Jewish messianic hope, which is reflected in such passages as Isa 9 and 11. The NT witness to Jesus as the Messiah involves a reinterpretation of the meaning of "kingship," in the light of the fact that Jesus had no political power. Nevertheless, the conventional idea of kingship has been retained in Christian tradition, in connection with Jesus, in the form of hope for his eschatological, royal triumph. Nor is the monarchial principle totally alien to the structures of authority among the modern people of God. The pope is certainly a monarch in the Roman Catholic Church, and there are dimensions of monarchy in the episcopal office of a number of contemporary denominations.

The mixed view of the monarchy in ancient Israel is presented best in the OT in the Books of Samuel. Here a positive assessment of the kingship as God's gift to his people (1 Sam 9:1 – 10:16; 2 Sam 7) stands in sharp contrast to a negative view of it as stiff-necked apostasy from the rule of God (1 Sam 8). The effect of this combination of texts in the story of Saul and David is to speak a "yes and no" to the monarchy as an instrument of order and well-being in Israel. This word takes its place alongside the unambiguous "yes" of the Psalms and the unambiguous "no" of Hosea as the third "biblical view" of kingship.

It would be a mistake to try to apply Hosea's oracles concerning the monarchy in any direct way to any modern com-

munity in which kingship is not the form of governance.
However, Hosea's analysis of the failure of the kingship in ancient Israel can provide us with the occasion to reflect upon
the proper forms and limits of power within our own communities, and upon the role of government within our life as a
people. On this latter issue, for example, there is a wide range
of opinion among Christians in America over the question of
the proper extent of involvement of government in health
care, education, and social welfare. Some take a negative view
of such involvement, regarding it as governmental interfer-
ence in people's lives, and a disavowal by individuals and
groups of the responsibility for their own well-being. Others
take a much more positive view of such involvement, seeing it
as a nation's way of providing services and opportunities
which individuals and groups cannot provide for themselves.
Of course, both opinions have been justified on the basis of
Christian moral principles. The responsibility of the modern
prophet in this sphere is not to decide between opposing opinions, but to help clarify the issues in the light of the biblical
understanding of God, humankind, and social responsibility.

One of the important points implied in Hosea's evaluation of Israel's diplomatic and military activity is that external means of this sort cannot remedy internal social and
moral ills. This issue is related to several that have been debated by religious leaders in recent years. For example, to
what extent can laws passed by the United States government
bring about equality of the races and sexes in American life?
Again, is violence a legitimate—and effective—instrument of
social change in highly stratified societies, like those in Latin
America? These questions relate to concrete situations which
are quite different from that of Israel in the eighth century
B.C., and we need to remain fully aware of these differences as
we try to apply the biblical message to modern life. Nevertheless, the larger ethical and theological issues with which
Hosea and his contemporaries struggled are related to issues
which we face in our own time.

God's Parental Love (11:1–11)

The love of God is the foundation and fulfillment of
Israel's life. Nowhere in the Bible is this conviction expressed
more clearly or memorably than in the eleventh chapter of

Hosea. In the seven preceding chapters we have been subject-
ed to a relentless assault upon the whole range of human iniq-
uities—Israel's, and by extension our own. Now, however, the
prophet returns to the themes which dominated the first three
chapters of the book, namely, the love of God and the covenantal history which is an expression of that love.

We have referred to the love of God which is described
here as parental rather than paternal. The dominant imagery
of God in the OT is masculine, and we have long been accustomed to refer to God as Father, both as an expression of our
own faith and as an appropriation of the language of the
Bible. However, the biblical images of God are not exclusively
masculine, and Hos 11 is a text which can be thought of equally well in either maternal or paternal terms. All of the acts of
nurturing described in this chapter are appropriate to both
mothers and fathers. For this reason the understanding of God
expressed in Hos 11 is even more adequate than that expressed in Hos 1 –3. The husband-wife metaphor which is
used to speak about God and Israel in chaps 1 –3 is a marvel-
ous vehicle for conveying the intimacy and passion of the di-
vine-human relationship. However, it lends itself, like so
many of the other biblical metaphors, to a sexist conception of
God. The parental metaphor which is the underlying image of
Hos 11 transcends the masculine-feminine dichotomy and is
therefore one of the most adequate symbols of God in the
Bible.

The story of love which is told in chap 11 is the same one
which undergirds the whole Book of Hosea. It is presented
most compactly here, and it is told in straightforward chronological sequence from beginning to end, that is to say, from
the past through the present to the future. In chap 2, the story
is told (using the husband-wife metaphor as we have said) in
twice as many words and in the sequence, present, past, future. The third presentation of this same basic understanding
of the history of Israel is to be found in chaps 12 –14. There,
however, the story is more an underlying structure of understanding than an explicit outline of the presentation itself.

The outline of Hosea's presentation of Israel's life-story
is quite simple, and it follows the outline of history with
which we are familiar from the Pentateuch. The sequence of
major events is as follows: God's deliverance of Israel in the

exodus from Egypt, divine guidance in the wilderness, the gift of the land as the place of Israel's settlement, Israel's apostasy from the God of the covenant, the fall and exile of the nation (conceived as a second captivity in Egypt), a second exodus and resettlement in the land in the new era of redemption. Thus it can be seen that Hosea uses the old story of Israel's covenantal history as a pattern for understanding the new era of Israel's life under God. At the moment when the prophet is addressing the nation it stands at a point of judgment and transition. The old era is drawing to a close and the new is about to begin. Even though the old era ends in punishment and loss, the whole is grounded in God's love, which aims at the fulfillment of his people's life in righteousness. The new era is grounded in this same love and is therefore filled with hope.

It may be useful to gather together here the passages which exhibit this basic structure of Hosea's understanding of Israel's history. In doing this we will use chap 11 as a framework within which to display the other materials.

The First Exodus-Wilderness Era. God redeemed the Israelites from Egypt and led them providentially in the wilderness:

"When Israel was a child, I loved him,
    and out of Egypt I called my son." (11:1)

"I am the Lord your God
    from the land of Egypt." (12:9)

"By a prophet the Lord brought Israel up from Egypt,
    and by a prophet he was preserved." (12:13)

"I am the Lord your God
    from the Land of Egypt;
you know no God but me,
    and besides me there is no savior." (13:4)

"Like grapes in the wilderness,
    I found Israel.
Like the first fruit on the fig tree,
    in its first season,
    I saw your fathers." (9:10)

"I led them with cords of compassion,

with the bands of love . . .
and I bent down to them and fed them." (11:4)

"It was I who knew you in the wilderness,
in the land of drought." (13:5)

"And there she shall answer as in the days of her youth,
as at the time when she came out of the land of
Egypt." (2:15)

The Settlement in Palestine. For Hosea the settlement was
a gift of God, and thus an event in the story of salvation; but it
was also the beginning of Israel's disobedience and idolatry:

"The more I called them,
the more they went from me;
they kept sacrificing to the Baals,
and burning incense to idols." (11:2)

"When they had fed to the full,
they were filled, and their heart was lifted up;
therefore they forgot me." (13:6)

"They came to Baal-peor,
and consecrated themselves to Baal." (9:10)

"Every evil of theirs is in Gilgal;
there I began to hate them." (9:15)

The era of apostasy and idolatry lasted from the time of settlement itself through the period of the monarchy, down to Hosea's own time. Most of the oracles in chaps 4 –10, and a good
part of 12 –13, deal with this aspect of Israel's story.

The Fall and Exile of the Nation. The old era is coming to
an end in punishment. This is represented as a return to captivity in Egypt, or as a second wandering in the wilderness.
However, it is not merely punishment. It is also a time of disci-
plining and moral renewal.

"They shall return to the land of Egypt,
and Assyria shall be their king,
because they have refused to return to me." (11:5)

"Their princes shall fall by the sword. . . .
This shall be their derision in the land of Egypt."
(7:16)

"Now he will remember their iniquity,
   and punish their sins;
   they shall return to Egypt." (8:13)

"They shall not remain in the land of the Lord;
   but Ephraim shall return to Egypt,
   and they shall eat unclean food in Assyria." (9:3)

"For behold they are going to Assyria;
   Egypt shall gather them,
   Memphis shall bury them." (9:6)

"Therefore, behold, I will allure her,
   and bring her into the wilderness,
   and speak tenderly to her." (2:14)

The New Exodus and Settlement in the Land. God will redeem Israel once again, as an expression of his abiding love.

"His sons shall come trembling from the west;
they shall come eagerly like birds from Egypt,
   and like doves from the land of Assyria;
   and I will return them to their homes, says the Lord."
   (11:10–11)

"I will heal their faithlessness;
   I will love them freely. . . .
They shall return and dwell beneath my shadow,
   they shall flourish as a garden." (14:4–7)

"And the people of Judah and the people of Israel shall be gathered together, and they shall appoint for themselves one head; and they shall go up from the land, for great shall be the day of Jezreel." (1:11)

"Afterward the children of Israel shall return and seek the Lord their God. . .; and they shall come in fear to the Lord and to his goodness in the latter days." (3:5)

"Therefore, behold, I will allure her,
   and bring her into the wilderness,
   and speak tenderly to her.
And there I will give her her vineyards,
   and make the valley of Achor a door of hope.
And there she shall answer as in the days of her youth,

as at the time when she came out of the land of
    Egypt. . . .
And I will make for them a covenant on that day . . .; and I
will betroth you to me forever; I will betroth you to me in
righteousness and in justice, in steadfast love, and in
mercy. I will betroth you to me in faithfulness; and you
shall know the Lord." (2:14 –20)

This synoptic presentation of key passages shows how
central the covenantal history is to the whole message of Hosea. It obviously plays a much larger role in his thought than
it does in Amos'. In this respect Hosea stands in close relationship to the Deuteronomic traditions reflected in the book of
Deuteronomy, the Deuteronomistic History (Joshua through
2 Kings), and the Book of Jeremiah. Jeremiah was deeply influenced by Hosea, and the editors of the Deuteronomic materials may have been, also. It is hard to know whether Hosea's
heavy reliance upon the covenantal history was one of the factors which led him to look beyond judgment to forgiveness
and redemption; however, one is inclined to suppose that this
was the case. Other factors have been treated in the Introduction to the Book of Hosea.

The tale told in Hos 11 is one of a parent's patient nurture
of a beloved child. Everything the parent does for the child is
motivated by love and the desire for the child to grow up to
responsible adulthood as a righteous and faithful child of God.
In the case of Israel this patient nurture failed. The child did
not respond appropriately to this love; therefore the parent
found it necessary to use sterner discipline, in order to bring
about the necessary learning and obedience. Up to this point
the prophet's use of the parent-child metaphor to describe the
history of Israel under God is quite compatible with our own
sensibilities. However, these sensibilities are shocked by the
next part of the story, as Hosea tells it, for here, in order to
continue using the metaphor, the prophet must ask us to
imagine the parent's using brutal disciplinary measures with
the child. The reason for this, of course, is that Hosea was really discussing the history of a nation, and the actual destiny
which he saw in store for the Kingdom of Israel was brutally
harsh. He was not suggesting that parents ought ever to be so
harsh in their treatment of their children. He was merely try-

ing to take the hard realities of Israel's life in the world of nations and interpret them in the light of the faith that this life
was ultimately based in the love and power of a living, personal God. It is impossible to speak about God, and God's relationship with the world, without using language and images
derived from human experience; but there is always the danger that such images will become fixed and absolute in our
thinking about God, with the result that the reality of God,
which transcends human comprehension, becomes distorted
in our minds.

Hosea believed God's love was stronger and more enduring than any human love, so that human love, even that
of a parent for a child, could only point to the divine reality;
it could not define its limits. "I am God and not man!" (11:9)
is the cry which the prophet puts in the mouth of God. In a
situation like the one Hosea described, human love would
be strained to the limit, and even exhausted. Israel, the
child of Yahweh, was incorrigible. The patient nurture of
God had been extended to the nation over a period of 500
years. No discipline had sufficed to bring about the kind of
covenantal obedience which God desired from his people,
and which was required if their corporate life was to be just
and good. What human parent or teacher could go on so
long without losing hope in the child's capacity to respond?
Eventually human love and patience are worn away, and
any further effort or concern is seen to be futile. But God's
love and patience are not like that. God persists forever. His
love is never exhausted.

Another facet of the divine love which sets it apart from
human love is that God does not deal with his creatures as
they deserve, but gives them gifts and opportunities far beyond their merit. God forgives even a hard-hearted and incorrigible people and seeks new ways to break through their self-
centeredness and lead them into a better way of life. This is
the message of the NT and it is also the message of the Book of
Hosea.

The parent-child metaphor, like any image derived from
human relationships, can lead to a distorted understanding of
God if it is absolutized or taken as a simple, literal description
of the activity of God. There is a related danger in using
human relationships like those of parent and child or husband

and wife to talk about peoples and nations. Nations are not like individual persons, and the course of a nation's history cannot be understood in the same terms as the life of an individual human being. If we fail to take account of the difference, we will make the same demands of nations—or churches—which we do of individuals, whether we do this explicitly or implicitly, and thus set ourselves up for disappointment and disillusionment. In the case of Israel in the eighth century B.C., it was possible for the nation, as defined by its political and cultic institutions, to be destroyed, while the people lived on to become the subjects of a new society. Hosea was confident that God could use the survivors of the fall of the Israelite Kingdom to create a new society. He did not distinguish between the people and the monarchial state; indeed, he uses the names Ephraim and Israel quite indiscriminately to refer to a whole range of interrelated but distinguishable entities. However, we must make these distinctions in trying to arrive at a clear understanding of the actual historical implications of Hosea's oracles, and in attempting to apply his faith to the circumstances of our own life.

The Patriarch as Archetype (12:1–15)

In discussing this chapter we will focus upon the feature which distinguishes it from the rest of the book, namely, the prophet's use of the Jacob-traditions. The concern with these traditions is new in the Book of Hosea. Elsewhere he relies heavily upon the story of Israel from the exodus to the settlement, but he makes very little reference to the patriarchal history. Here in chap 12, by contrast, the figure of Jacob dominates the presentation. Although this much is clear, there are many details in the chapter which are obscure. An examination of the modern translations and commentaries will show that the Hebrew text of this chapter is very difficult indeed, and that there is significant disagreement among scholars as to the interpretation of Jacob which is presented here. Without going into detail, we may note that there are two principal schools of thought on this subject. One takes the picture of Jacob in the chapter as favorable, at least in part, while the other regards it as entirely unfavorable. The latter view seems to me to be correct, and it is the one we will follow here. Because of the textual difficulties involved, any interpretation of Hos 12 must be tentative.

The Jacob of Hos 12 is self-seeking, greedy, dishonest, and cruel. He is a totally unsavory character. In this there is some similarity with the picture of Jacob in Genesis. However, in Genesis his character is morally ambiguous, whereas here in Hosea he has no redeeming traits at all. Hosea may have selected only those features of the patriarch which he wished to stress in order to make his rhetorical point. However, it is also possible that the Jacob traditions as he knew them differed somewhat from those which we have in the Bible as it has come to us. We must remember that the Bible as we know it had not yet taken shape in Hosea's time. Furthermore, the Bible as it has come down to us is a substantially Judean book. It is heavily weighted with materials reflecting the experience of the Kingdom of Judah, and the entire OT has been edited in a Judean perspective. From all that we can infer about Hosea from his oracles, he was an Ephraimite and a subject of the northern Kingdom of Israel. Despite the occasional references to Judah in the Book of Hosea, most of which appear to be editorial comments added by a later Judean scribe, Hosea appears to have addressed his oracles to the leaders and people of the northern kingdom, and the religious traditions which he draws upon seem to have differed somewhat in detail and perspective from the Judean traditions which now dominate the OT story.

Whatever may have been the literary antecedents of Hosea's oracles, the point that he is making in chap 12 is clear. The tribe of Ephraim of the eighth century, that is, the prophet's audience, is an exact replica of its ancestor Jacob, the conniving, selfish cheat! Elsewhere in the book we have seen how he traced the institutions of the monarchy and the sacrificial cultus back to their earliest beginnings in Israel's life, in order to assert that the two were evil in root and branch. In this case the historical continuity was traced from the event of the crossing into the land of western Palestine at Gilgal, and the establishment of the monarchy at Gibeah. Now, however, Hosea personalizes the comparison between the behavior of the present generation and that of the ancestors by employing the figure of Jacob. As we move through the chapter it becomes evident that Jacob represents both the ancient figure of the patriarch and the current generation of Ephraimites. What makes them alike is not the similarity of their outward way of life, for that had changed a great deal in the thousand years between the age of the patriarchs and the age of Hosea, but rather the similarity of disposition and motive. The ancestor and his distant progeny were flawed in the same way. They were uncommitted to the corporate good of the people, and were dedicated to their own selfish gain. This is not a pretty picture, but Hosea did not intend to please or entertain his audience. He prophesied at a time of grave moral and social danger for his people, and he was uncompromisingly candid in his analysis of their behavior.

It is difficult to find parallels in our own cultural and religious traditions to Hosea's use of the figure of Jacob in these oracles. We remember the heroes in our ancestry and forget the villains. Even the heroes tend to be recalled as unambiguously good, rather than as persons of mixed motive and imperfect behavior. Of course, Jacob was a hero to Hosea's audience, and not a villain. It was Hosea's reinterpretation of the ancestor that made Jacob perverse. When writers in our own time "debunk" our heroes, they are not trying to use the revised portrait as a means of showing us the archetype of our own iniquity. Nevertheless, perhaps we can perform this service for ourselves by making a candid assessment of those model figures in our past with whom we would like to identify. One of the reasons why we have heroes is to exalt ourselves by identifying with them, and sharing vicariously in their triumphs. When we acknowledge that they had divided hearts, just as we do, we are better prepared to acknowledge our own moral failures and take the necessary steps to set our affairs aright. It may be important to have heroes at a certain stage in one's life, but it is equally important to appraise them objectively at a later stage. The achievement of moral maturity requires this kind of candor, both about the archetypes which serve as our models and about ourselves.

The Death of a Kingdom (13:1–16)

"O death, where is your sting!" asked the apostle Paul, alluding to Hos 13:14 (1 Cor 15:55). The answer to the question for Paul, of course, was that death had no sting because God had overcome it through the resurrection of Jesus Christ. The

Greek translation of Hos 13, which Paul used, lent itself to this interpretation. Nevertheless, it involves a reversal of the thrust of the passage in the prophetic oracle itself. This is not to say that there was anything wrong with Paul's theology, but only that his use of the passage from Hosea cannot guide us in our understanding of the original intention of the text. Hosea's meaning was quite different. Indeed, it was so different as to be shocking to the Christian reader of the Bible.

Hos 13:14 should be translated as follows:

> "Shall I ransom them from the power of Sheol?
> Shall I deliver them from death?
> I am your pestilence, O Death!
> I am your plague, O Sheol!
> Repentance is hid from my eyes!"

The marginal notes in most of the modern versions of the Bible make it possible for the English reader to discern something of the shape of the Hebrew text and to realize why the modern translators were embarrassed by it. In fact, the modern versions represent a bowdlerizing of Hosea's oracle. Hosea himself uttered this bold, terrifying statement at the climax of the most terrible oracle in the book. He characterized God as the dark destroyer, the pestilence of death, the plague of the underworld! I believe we should take this prophetic statement seriously and not try to explain it away.

Hosea was describing the death of the Kingdom of Israel. He was absolutely convinced that it was about to take place, and he was equally convinced that it had been brought about by the sin and stupidity of the nation, particularly its royal and cultic leadership. But if the cause of destruction was the iniquity of the kingdom, and the instrument, the army of Assyria, the agent was God.

The destruction of a kingdom is not a pretty thing. The horrors which Hosea describes in chap 13 are not the inventions of a misanthropic poet, but the observations of a sober student of human affairs. War is filled with atrocities. The ones described in Hos 13 are typical of both ancient and modern times. Hardly a month passes that we are not shown such pictures by the news media. Therefore, we do not question the accuracy of Hosea's account. Our problem is not with his description of what would happen to Israel if she were conquered, but with his interpretation of the event as an act of

God. This problem is put in its starkest form by the lines which we have quoted above. What are we to make of this terrible assertion? Is God really the bringer of such destruction?

The theological issue is that of human freedom and divine providence. To what extent is it legitimate to discern the hand of God in the events of history? The OT writers regarded them as being under the immediate control of God, and manifesting his response to the moral worth of human behavior. However, many people in the modern world reject such a view, believing that events in history are entirely the result of human action, or the interaction of human beings with the natural environment. For these people, there is no need to attribute anything that happens to divine intervention. Furthermore, for many modern religious people it is theologically untenable to attribute any direct responsibility to God for much of what happens in history. For them, the love of God is incompatible with such things as the extermination of Jews in the twentieth century or the slaughter of Israelite women in the eighth century B.C. (Hos 13:16). The blame for such atrocities would have to be laid entirely at the feet of human beings.

In order to be fair to the OT tradition, we must acknowledge that it does not present a completely unified interpretation of history. Voices were raised by some of the biblical writers to protest against a simple moral explanation of the fortunes of people's lives. The most powerful of these voices was that of the writer of the Book of Job. Using the folk-hero Job as an example, he shows that what happens in human history cannot always be explained as a divine punishment for sin or reward for righteousness. Job's affliction resulted from a combination of physical and social forces. The writer did not distinguish between the two types of agency, as we would be inclined to do. The effect of his protest, then, was to challenge the traditional Israelite belief that events both in nature and in history are direct manifestations of the rewards and punishments of God. The writer of Job was concerned to deny that prosperity and affliction in human life were reward for human virtue and punishment for human iniquity, meted out directly by God. He was not concerned to explain how prosperity and affliction actually come about. Neither he nor the other biblical writers thought to analyze the processes and events which transpire in nature and history as the result of the interaction of creatures, human and sub-human, that are more or less free and self-motivated. However, the understanding of the relationship between God and humankind which is presented in the Book of Job is compatible with this modern description of our physical and social environment. The theological question is not how creation operates, but whether the creator manipulates it in order to reward and punish human beings. I believe that God does not do this and that this conviction is essentially the same as the one expressed by the writer of Job. This conviction is also supported by the famous teaching of Jesus that God "makes his sun rise on the evil and on the good, and sends rain on the just and on the unjust" (Matt 5:45).

What, then, can we say about a biblical passage like the thirteenth chapter of Hosea? I think that we should admit at the outset that the destruction of the Kingdom of Israel, which involved the slaughter of many innocent people, was prophesied by Hosea as if it were a direct punishment of God. However, we cannot and need not accept his account as a sufficient explanation of the event. As an analysis of the cause of the destruction, it is clearly deficient. Nevertheless, we can make sense of his proclamation in the context of his public ministry, and we can be stimulated by it to ask important questions about the meaning of events in our own time.

If the primary audience of Hosea's oracles was the leadership of the Kingdom of Israel, as seems reasonable to suppose, then his prophecy of the destruction of Israel served as an invitation to them to reflect upon the part which they played in shaping the nation's destiny. The oracle could serve this purpose even though it contained an oversimplified interpretation of that history. After all, the prophet was engaged in rhetoric, not scientific historiography. After the fall of the nation, the prophet's oracles continued to provide the occasion for the surviving elders of Israel to reflect upon the meaning of their experience and their responsibilities for the future. Something like this can also take place in our reflection upon events in our own time. We do not need to be able to give a full account of the causes of historical events in order to be able to learn from them. The Jewish holocaust is a case in point. It is difficult to explain, or understand, how such a thing could happen. However, we do not have to explain it in order to be able to respond to it. It can be a powerful spur to the reexamination of our attitudes and values and to a new commitment to the cause of human rights and religious toleration. God was not responsible for the extermination of millions of Jews. The holocaust was not an act of God, nor an expression of the will of God. However, it serves as the occasion for the people of God to ponder the meaning of their life amidst the peoples of the world, in the light of what they understand to be the will of God. It seems to me that this is the proper way for a religious community to deal with the tragic events of history. A literalistic adoption of the interpretive model provided by the oracles of the prophets creates far more problems for our religious understanding than it solves. It is not a constructive way to appropriate the prophetic message.

New Life for a People (14:1– 9)

Nothing can prevent the eventual triumph of God's love. This is the overarching message of the Book of Hosea. Therefore, it is appropriate that it should be reaffirmed in the concluding oracle.

The message of redemption and hope which closes the book stands in stark contrast to the prophecy of desolation and death which stands in the preceding chapter. Chap 13 should never be taken by itself. At best it is a partial word. The biblical proclamation, which begins with the good news of God's salvation, concludes with an expression of hope, the reaffirmation of the saving love of God, which is the ground and end of human life.

The last four chapters provide an outline of Hosea's theology of history. Chap 11 affirms God's nurturing love, which is the basis of redemption and of the entire covenantal history of Israel. Chap 12 focuses upon Israel's apostasy. Chap 13 is all about doom, which is the consequence of apostasy. Chap 14 proclaims the re-creation of the people of God beyond the era of doom. Thus the message of chaps 11– 14 is the same as chaps 1– 3, although it is cast in different words and images.

Hos 14 opens with a call to repentance: "Return, O Israel, to the Lord your God" (14:1)! Israel had lost her way, down strange roads with alien gods. Eventually she would have to return in order to find true life. Her discipline would be severe. It would involve the loss of her political and cultic institutions, her self-determination, and possession of her ancestral land. Many of her people would be deported and forced to live among strange people and alien cultures. All other forms of discipline had failed to produce the kind of religious fidelity and corporate righteousness which are the root and branch of covenantal existence. Therefore, Israel would have to suffer the harsh discipline which the prophet foresaw. Nevertheless, the ultimate goal of divine discipline was education and re-creation.

Moral renewal requires a free decision. Obedience must be willing or it is not fully human. Love is a gift, an invitation, and it must be answered freely, willingly, in love. Forced compliance is not true obedience. Therefore, after the discipline, which *can* be imposed against the will, there is the invitation to return.

Israel's turning to God always involves worship. It is possible for an individual to be religious without participating in corporate worship. However, it is not possible for Israel to exist as the people of God unless its life is formed by the public worship of God. This was true of the Israel of old and it is equally true of the several communities which draw their life from the biblical tradition. For preexilic Israel the public worship of God put heavy stress upon the system of animal sacrifices. When administered and understood properly, this system contributed positively to the religious life of Israel. However, it was subject to easy abuse. It could be degraded into magic and idolatry by the misunderstanding of the people and the manipulation of the priests. Hosea, like Amos and the other preexilic prophets, was a relentless critic of this abuse. Indeed, in his eyes the sacrificial system as it had come to be practiced in Israel was one of the principal obstacles in the way of Israel's true covenantal obedience. Therefore, when he turns toward the future to describe the worship of God which the renewed people of Israel will perform, he depicts a ritual of the altar that is completely transformed. In place of the liturgy of blood sacrifice there is only a liturgy of words (14:2). Hosea admonishes the new Israel to "Take with you words and return to the Lord," and they reply, "We will render the bulls of our lips." This is a literal translation of the Hebrew text, and it makes excellent sense. The only bulls which Israel will offer to the Lord in the ritual of the new era are the symbolical bulls of their lips. The old manipulation of the blood of beasts will have been replaced by a liturgy of prayer and praise.

There was ample precedent in the worship of preexilic Israel for the ritual of words which Hosea prophesied for the new era. The Book of Psalms contains a rich legacy of confession, thanksgiving, petition and praise from the preexilic sanctuaries of Israel. But in that era songs and prayers were accompanied by animal sacrifices. In Hosea's vision of the new era these sacrifices would not be performed. He does not spell out what he had in mind, nor does he prescribe in detail what form a new liturgy of the word might take. It would be reading far too much into Hosea's brief poetic allusion to see in it the idea of the synagogue, which developed in Judaism after the exile. Nevertheless, there is the seed of such an idea in Hosea's prophecy.

So, no sacrificial bulls! Furthermore, in the new Israel there would be no reliance upon foreign nations for salvation, and no idolatry (14:3). Not relying on Assyria, or some other power, for salvation does not mean political isolationism. It means not expecting foreign alliances to create the kind of society which is the goal of covenantal obedience.

Two points more are made in this concluding oracle of the book. The first is that God will heal his people's faithlessness (14:4), and the second is that Israel will flourish in the garden of God (14:5–7). The love of God is not a reward for human righteousness. It is a healing power which makes righteousness possible. It precedes and undergirds all human effort, and it makes all striving for extraneous reward unnecessary and undesirable. "We love because he first loved us" is the message of Hosea, as well as the NT.

At the end of his oracle Hosea shows us a kind of Eden restored. Some commentators have regarded this picture as un-Hosean, indeed unprophetic, because it deals with material, rather than moral, blessedness. To be sure, Hosea, like all the prophets, put moral and religious values above material ones. However, the proper enjoyment of the goodness of the created world was part of God's intention for all people, according to the consistent testimony of the OT writers. Furthermore, Hos 14:5–7 is matched by 2:21–23. Both of these great promises of renewal affirm the unity of created life, of body and spirit, of world and word. God is sovereign over the whole of creation, and the blessings he lavishes upon his people are both "material" and "spiritual." Actually, these are dangerous terms to use, for they imply a dichotomy between the outer and inner aspects of being, and thus distort the biblical perspective as well as our own experience. All creation is derived from God and must serve his loving purpose in the end. However we may distinguish between matter and mind, both should be valued as God's creation.

Hos 14:1–7 is not a blueprint for a future society. It says nothing about the political or religious institutions which would be necessary to give order to Israel's life. For the most part the OT prophets avoided trying to predict what these might be. Occasionally they prophesied the restoration of the Davidic monarchy, as the editor of Hosea did in Hos 3:5 (cf. Jer 33:14–26). More often they kept silent before the mystery of the future. They had faith that God would recreate his covenantal people, and they expressed this faith in poetic figures like those in Hosea's closing oracle. The exact shape of the future they left to the freedom and righteousness of God.

Bibliography

The articles on Amos and Hosea in the *Interpreter's Dictionary of the Bible* and the *Supplementary Volume* to this dictionary provide good introductory essays and bibliographic material on these prophets.

There are a number of good studies on the message and theology of these two prophets: Walter Breuggemann, *Tradition for Crisis: A Study in Hosea* (Atlanta: John Knox Press, 1968); Bernhard W. Anderson, *The Eighth Century Prophets* (Proclamation Commentaries; Philadelphia: Fortress Press, 1978); and Robert B. Coote, *Amos Among the Prophets* (Philadelphia: Fortress Press, 1981). See also my *Amos and Isaiah* (Nashville: Abingdon Press; 1969).

Among the various commentaries on these prophetical books, the following are most useful for the minister: James L. Mays, *Amos* (Philadelphia: Westminster Press, 1969) and *Hosea* (Philadelphia: Westminster Press, 1969); H. W. Wolff, *Joel and Amos* (Philadelphia: Fortress Press, 1977) and *Hosea* (Philadelphia: Fortress Press, 1974); and Francis I. Andersen and David Noel Freedman, *Hosea* (Anchor Bible; Garden City: Doubleday, 1980). See also my *Hosea* (New York: Harper & Row, 1966).